BLOSSOMS IN THE DUST

DUST

The Human Factor in Indian Development

by

KUSUM NAIR

Foreword by

GUNNAR MYRDAL

F   *her*

BOOKS THAT MATTER

915.4
N14b
62547
August 1968

Published in the United States of America in 1962
by Frederick A. Praeger, Inc., Publisher
64 University Place, New York 3, N.Y.

© KUSUM NAIR 1961

Library of Congress Catalog Card Number: 62-13492

PRINTED IN GREAT BRITAIN

FOR
ARUNA AND KAPIL

CONTENTS

MAHARASHTRA AND HIMACHAL PRADESH

GUJERAT

THE LAST CHAPTER

ILLUSTRATIONS

FOREWORD

As the Prime Minister of India, Jawaharlal Nehru, never ceases to stress, the problem facing his country after winning political independence is how to bring about a social and economic revolution by peaceful means. India is resolutely moulding all her public life, from the national down to the local level, in the framework of democracy with universal suffrage. The hope is that reform, amounting to a total remaking of social and economic relations, shall be carried out by the people themselves, with a minimum of direction from above and without resort to compulsion.

The reforms need to be planned. The idea is that the planning should be democratic, not only in the sense that it is done for the people and sets the welfare of the masses as its supreme goal. It should be done by the people—should be steered by, and express, their desires, ambitions and needs. It must rely upon them for political backing and, since compulsion is excluded, also for giving effect to the policies contained in the Plan. In the final instance, Indian democratic planning aims at initiating a social process, within which the masses of people become increasingly motivated to strive for improving their lot as individuals and, at the same time, for improving society by co-operative endeavour.

The human factor in development thus becomes of paramount importance. Does the will to individual progress and co-operation exist among the masses, or can it be released and activated? Many of the best friends of India in the Western countries often speak as if they believed that the several hundreds of millions of people in the villages and the towns are now standing up to take their destiny in their own hands, ready to rise out of long ages of stagnation and destitution, determined to create a better life for themselves by individual and collective effort. The expression which has been given

such wide currency in recent years, "the revolution of rising expectations", is often used to convey the same thought. Those, who
carry the responsibility to give life and reality to India's ambitious
development policies are, of course, aware that the problem is a much
more difficult one.

People's attitudes to work and life, hardened by stagnation, isolation, ignorance and poverty, and underpinned by tradition and often
by religion, are frequently found to be inimical to change of any kind.
As this book illustrates, the situation varies in regions and communities in the vast realm that is India. But people, even, and not
least, the poorest people, often set their sights, not upon individual
progress, but upon mere survival, and then they can still less be
expected to have the inclination, and the daring, to aim at an inten-
tional, concerted, co-operative effort to remake society. Until this
whole system of traditional attitudes has been changed there is a frail
basis for democratic planning in the Indian sense. For, to have
development only in some sections, while others are lagging is contrary to the aims of that planning. India wants the entire nation to
advance. It aspires to greater equality and broader sharing in ideas
as well as accomplishments.

Largely influenced by Marxian ideas about the "processes of
production" as the ultimate determinants of all that is culture, we of
the present age place perhaps too much reliance upon industrializa-
tion. Modernization in this one field is assumed to initiate change in
the entire society. But the question is how rapidly and strongly this
influence really works. As a rule, the spread effects, from a point of
induced expansion, are for various reasons weak in a very poor
country, while there are sometimes backwash effects actually im-
poverishing the surrounding sectors. In India the danger has been
clearly seen that the new industries may remain enclaves, as in
colonial times, and result in a "dual economy", and that, in particular, the larger part of the country, which is rural, might remain
backward. This is the motivation for the valiant policies of the Indian
Government directed towards changing the countryside: community
development and the co-operative movement, agricultural extension
work, and, of course, the raising of the levels of education and health,
etc. Their aim is to attack the development problems of rural India
on that deeper level of human attitudes and social relations.

While starting new large-scale industries and building dams, power
installations and other overhead facilities certainly have their diffi-

culties in an underdeveloped country, those are small compared with the difficulties meeting these attempts to change and radically improve the attitudes to life and work of the people in the villages, and the social structures into which the attitudes are moulded. The earnest and continual efforts to ascertain the results of these policies, to evaluate them critically, both by the agencies of the Government and by independent researchers, belong to the things that India today can most rightly be proud of. Policies do not become frozen, but are insistently put up to critical re-examination.

This book is an individual contribution in this same direction. The author, who is an anxious citizen of new India and shares its fundamental values and ambitions, spent a year walking around in the villages, talking to the people about what was on their mind; she devoted one more year to sorting out from her copious field notes—36 bulky volumes—what little could find place in a volume, where she also had to give space to some background information. She tried to keep back her own ideas and preconceptions, and to let the people she met enlarge upon their own worries. The lead she gave by her questions represents, however, an approach; this approach, which is identical with the accepted line that India should develop by means of democratic planning, she defines in the Preface and the Introduction. In the last chapter, she has formulated some of her tentative conclusions.

I had the occasion to discuss her experiences in the field at an early stage of her project, and I have, like several of my Indian and Western friends and colleagues, seen in manuscript even more of her material than could find place in the present volume. I am only stressing a consensus of opinion when I express the hope that this important little book will find many readers. It is primarily a literary work bringing home to us that which statistical and other surveys cannot do equally forcefully and vividly, viz. what folkways and folk-thoughts are in the villages—or, rather, in some villages, as India is so vast. In India itself, her book will contribute to strengthening those who are pleading for a greater emphasis on the human factor in development. Abroad, it will make people better realize the true scope of the problems and the immense difficulties India has to face. Nothing is won in sympathy, and much may be lost, by the facile and false optimism which sometimes passes as good publicity. Struggling India—Government and people—deserves to be seen and understood as she really is.

Out of this more realistic perception should come, both in India and abroad, the will and courage that is the reverse of indifference and complacency. On the very last page the author has a sentence that I want to quote here, as I believe it is important for the reader to see it before he reads the book: "I can clearly assert that the experience of my travels and contacts with the village communities has not given me any sense of pessimism or defeatism."

I would, at last, want to express my hope that the author will find time and opportunity to enlarge upon her theme in some form or another, to present her material more fully, and in the context of other material which is available and continually becoming available from all the evaluation work that is going on, and then also go further in the analytical appraisal of the facts she has observed.

Stockholm, January 1961.

GUNNAR MYRDAL

AUTHOR'S PREFACE

In making this survey I travelled through India continuously for one year, mostly by road, starting in August 1958. I toured all the States of India except Jammu and Kashmir, Tripura and the Andaman and Nicobar Islands.

In each State I selected three or four, sometimes more, districts. A district in India is generally the basic unit of civil administration. In each district, I chose a number of typical villages, taking into account certain factors, such as the physical situation of the hamlet and the size and composition of its population.

In most cases, I went into a village without any previous intimation, introduced myself and explained the purpose of my visit, and then settled down to a long talk in groups or singly. I had no set questionnaire. I would allow the conversation to develop naturally, giving it only a minimum of direction to keep it more or less on the subject of the dominant development project or problem of the locality. But the overall approach remained uniform throughout: to assess the impact of development upon the individuals and communities involved.

I took notes on the spot, recording all conversations verbatim. There may be an occasional error in the spelling of names or places due to the difficulties of transcribing them into Roman characters. And despite my best efforts there may be some errors in the statistics. In the villages especially, it is practically impossible to be certain about the accuracy of figures; they are always approximate. Also, there are serious limitations affecting the accuracy of official statistical data. But none of these factors would significantly alter or distort the overall picture in which we are interested. The statistical evidence contained in the book is only incidental to the main findings.

As to the accuracy of what the people told me—it is fairly easy in

a village to determine this. In the first place, a collective lie is difficult unless pre-arranged. This was obviated by my visiting the villages in most cases without any previous warning. Besides, I always
visited several villages in the same area and so could check what the
residents of one village said against the rest. Above all, I had the
advantage of being not only a native but a "nobody". I was not a
government official, a politician, or public figure. I could do the
villagers no harm, nor could I bestow any favours. This made it
easier to win their confidence and to persuade them to speak frankly.
The Indian peasant is generally friendly, and if he is convinced of
the visitor's sincerity and *bona fides*, he usually responds in like
fashion.

Even so, I took special care to check what the people said and my
impressions of them and of the facts of a particular situation against
every other available source, such as official records and surveys,
officials of the local and State administration and other knowledge-
able elements in the local population, such as teachers, lawyers,
politicians, social workers and so on.

To avoid repetition and to meet the publisher's wishes about the
size of the book, I have selected for inclusion only a small portion of
the material collected, but I have sought to ensure that what is given
is representative of the people and a region on a sufficiently significant scale to deserve notice.

The treatment is narrative and descriptive rather than analytic.
This manner is better suited for bringing out the attitudes and
opinions of the people interviewed, as well as some glimpses of their
background and environment, which are perhaps important for a
clearer appreciation.

In many areas, particularly in the southern and eastern States, I
had to converse through an interpreter. That was an unavoidable
limitation. India has fourteen officially recognized languages besides
a number of dialects, and I know only very few. This made it impossible to translate them literally, and to convey the flavour of the
regional and class variations in their speech.

A glossary of Hindi words has been provided for the foreign
reader.

I may add here that certain terms used in the text of this book have
perhaps a slightly different connotation in the west. Thus the word
"tenant" often indicates what is understood as a tenant in the
western countries, as well as a share-cropper. The words "culti-

vator" and "agriculturist" do not imply that the peasant necessarily tills the land himself. They may merely indicate that he lives mainly by income from agriculture. Then there are certain communities in India that are agriculturist by caste. They are like the other professional castes, such as those of blacksmiths or weavers. The majority of the people who actually work on the land belong to what are known as the scheduled castes or *Harijans*. They are normally landless and work as hired hands or share-croppers.

Finally, I acknowledge herewith, my very deep gratitude and most earnest thanks to all who helped me and made the writing of this book possible. This includes the many friends, some of them eminent scholars, who have been so generous with their time and extremely valuable advice, criticism and suggestions. My sincere thanks extend also to the men and women whom I met in the villages during my travels, who form the subject of this book and provide its characters. Nothing but pleasant memories, though often tinged with sadness, survive in my mind of those thousands of hours of talks and discussions—of the good humour, the kind, at times overwhelming hospitality, the remarkable dignity and courage, despite the mud walls and the often empty cooking utensils. But for their willing cooperation, interest and help I could never have succeeded in this undertaking.

New Delhi   KUSUM NAIR

January 1961

INTRODUCTION

On the stroke of midnight on 14th August, 1947, the Tricolour was hoisted to the strains of the national anthem. India became independent.

The monsoon night was starless but aglow with the brilliant illuminations below. Every man, woman and child was out to witness the supreme, historic moment and the air was filled with jubilant cries of *"Jai Hind!"*.

An elemental force had burst its confines and swept like a flood across the land. Would it also wash away the cobwebs, the inertia and deadness of centuries? Would it create overnight a brave new country in which everything would be perfect? Anything seemed possible.

Next morning, the sun rose in the eastern sky to reveal the same squalor, the staggering poverty and hunger, the deep inequalities as the day before. Myriads of flowers, yellow and orange marigolds and pink rose petals, lay scattered on the ground, stale, scentless, trampled.

The municipal sweepers came and swept the streets, and the blossoms mingled in the dust.

2

An age and a journey had ended. In the same moment, however, another had begun.

Of the momentous events in the decade following independence, perhaps one of the most important in the long term perspective was the decision of the Indian Government to direct and regulate the pattern and tempo of future economic development in the country by state planning, followed by a declaration by the Indian Parliament, in December 1954, that the broad objective of economic policy should be to achieve a "socialist pattern of society".

A national Planning Commission was established in 1950, which drew up the first of a series of Five Year Plans, for the period commencing in April 1951. In the context of the economic backwardness in which India found herself at the time of independence, and in view of the parliamentary system of democracy which she adopted, the boldness and magnitude of these Five Year Plans is impressive and perhaps unique. But so of course are the problems, complex and staggering in their immensity.

Nevertheless, achievements in the economic field have been impressive. The increase in national income, for example, in the First Plan is estimated to have been 18 per cent, though the Second Plan represented a larger and more broad-based effort. At the end of the Second Plan period, national income (at constant prices) is expected to have increased by about 42 per cent, per capita income by about 20 per cent, and per capita consumption by about 16 per cent over the decade 1951–61.[1] The foundations of the Indian economy have been considerably strengthened, especially the industrial base.

Thus, three new steel plants have been constructed, increasing the finished steel capacity to 4.5 million tons as compared to 1.3 million tons at the beginning of the Second Plan period, while industrial production in 1960–61 is expected to be more than double the level of 1950–51. Much more rapid expansion is contemplated in the Third Plan period (1961–66), when an investment of more than Rs. 10,000 *crores* is envisaged, as compared with a total investment of Rs. 3,360 *crores* in the First Plan and of Rs. 6,750 *crores* in the Second.

3

The central objective of planning in India at the present stage was defined in the First Plan: "to initiate a process of development which will raise living standards and open out to the people new opportunities for a richer and more varied life. The problem of development of an under-developed economy is one of utilizing more effectively the potential resources available to the community, and it is this which involves economic planning. But the economic condition

---

[1] All statistics quoted in this section are drawn from the *Third Five Year Plan, A Draft Outline*, Planning Commission, Govt. of India, June 1960.

of a country at any given time is a product of the broader social environment. . . ."[1]

It was to discover this "broader social environment" in its economic context and implications, to try to find out what is the impact of deliberate development on the individual men and women who make up India's millions, that I undertook this project.

I confined myself to the rural sector for many reasons. Agriculture embraces nearly 70 per cent of the country's population and it occupies a position of highest priority in the overall scheme of national growth and development in the Five Year Plans. Apart from the larger long-term problem of improving the living standards of the masses engaged in agriculture, the country's food production must be increased substantially in order merely to wipe out the existing deficit and to keep pace with the rapid growth in population. The present short-fall in production of food and of several raw materials, such as cotton, costs the country dearly in scarce foreign exchange and adds to inflationary pressures.

Average crop yields in India are among the lowest in the world, and it is believed that productivity cannot be improved unless the millions of peasants that make up the Indian farming community are persuaded to adopt more scientific techniques of cultivation. A widespread and costly effort is therefore being made by the government to bring about a sweeping technological revolution in the agricultural field and accompanying institutional changes in rural society.

Very little, however, is known at first hand about the farmer himself, the key actor in the democratic and planned revolution that is under way in this country. Little is known about his personality, motivations and attitudes, or even the real conditions of his life. There is sufficient statistical data to permit some generalizations about him. But his attitudes and motivations in the specific context of the technological changes and economic development being planned for him by the government have been relatively little investigated. Yet the success or failure of the efforts to change the conditions of the peasant's life and methods of work is of crucial concern to India, and indeed to the world.

[1] *The First Five Year Plan*, Planning Commission, New Delhi, p. 7.

4

I have tried to depict as full and representative a picture as possible of the human situation as it obtains in the country's rural society. It does not pertain to a date in any particular year but is true of the era, of the post-independence period. To those engaged in working on problems and programmes of development, it will, I hope, help to bring about a clearer appreciation of the nature and immense complexity of the factors involved in planning for change and economic growth in India's agriculture.

Not a single character, situation or statement in the whole book is fictitious, contrived, exaggerated—or, for that matter, understated. I have reported the situation as I came upon it and, to the best of my ability, *as it appeared to the man at the other end*. Even where the people I talked with failed palpably to understand the magnitude and meaning of events or to interpret correctly the intentions underlying an official policy, I have reported their reactions factually, because the important thing in a situation is not always what it is, but what it appears to be to those immediately concerned. The beliefs that people hold condition their understanding of a situation as well as their attitudes and actions, and thus they affect the pace and direction of development in any field.

But people do not always believe what they should believe or are expected to believe. Their beliefs are often obsolete—the products of dogma and tradition the reasons for which have long ceased to exist. It may sometimes be easier to build a million-ton steel plant—with borrowed money and hired know-how, if necessary—than to change a man's outlook on such matters as the use of irrigation water, fertilizer or contraceptives. It is necessary, therefore, to be fully acquainted with the prevailing value systems underlying the behaviour patterns in any human community if one is to understand the nature of the factors likely to be involved in that community's economic growth and development.

I have added a chapter at the end in which I have outlined briefly my own analysis and interpretation of the mass of purely empirical data contained in the main text. This, I hope, will be useful and suggestive without deterring the reader from reaching his own conclusions.

5

The material presented in this book highlights a number of interesting sociological problems deserving of further examination. We are, however, not concerned with these problems *per se*, but only in so far as they have a bearing on processes of change involved in induced economic growth in a traditional rural society. On the other hand, no attempt has been made to assess or evaluate the physical achievements of the Plans or of any specific projects. Where specific schemes and development projects do appear they only provide the backdrop and the context of the human element involved in the implementation and fulfilment of those schemes.

Many of my accounts may seem to the foreigner, and even to the Indian reader, to be contrary to general expectations and out of focus in the larger perspective of the ideals and the image of future India as conceived by the country's intellectual and political leaders. But then a worm's vision can scarcely be expected to coincide with that of its Creator, and this book reports the point of view *only* of a number of the most common people, generally described as the rural masses, who are immersed in purely local and immediate interests, are generally unaware of larger issues, and are most of them illiterate as the wind.

Nonetheless, they constitute the largest section of India's population and the very core of its present planning. It is precisely their local pursuits and problems that add up to the basic problems of the country, and it is ultimately their attitude to a scheme or project which must determine the measure of its success or failure.

As in every country, so in India also, there are certain subjects, such as caste and untouchability, which seem sometimes to be considered taboo outside scholarly surveys. They are not normally mentioned in polite society. One reason is often the fear of being misquoted or misunderstood by foreigners. I have, however, described them as I found them, because I believe they have important economic implications which must be faced if effective solutions are to be found. To avoid facing unpleasant facts is self-defeating and could be dangerous. What I have written is in all sincerity, in a humble spirit of scientific enquiry and accurate reporting, without any malice or prejudice toward the people of any region or community. I trust that it will be taken by the reader in the same spirit of objectivity.

In my travels I found much that was heartening and encouraging, but also much that was discouraging. I did not set out to prove or disprove any pre-conceived premises or theories, but I have not tried to suppress facts because they are unpleasant. Some words that Alfred Marshall once wrote seem appropriate:

"Students of social science must fear popular approval; evil is with them, when all men speak well of them. . . . It is almost impossible for a student to be a true patriot and have the reputation of being one at the same time."[1]

[1] From an unpublished manuscript in *Memorials of Alfred Marshall*, p. 89.

MADRAS

CHAPTER I

RICE-GIRDLED HORIZONS

"Here in Tanjore, a man owning even one acre of land calls himself a *mirasdar*. He will never go to the field and work with his own hands", a group of young *mirasdars* explain to me in fluent English, in their village of Agavamangudi. "This is the land of 'gentlemen' farmers."

A deltaic tract of the river Cauvery, in the southern State of Madras, the whole district of Tanjore is highly fertile. It is in fact the granary of Madras—its rice bowl. More paddy is cultivated here than in any other district in the State, and large quantities are exported. Irrigated lands, which are extensive, grow two consecutive crops of it. For miles on end, in all directions, one sees nothing but paddy.

The outcome of this fortuitous state of circumstances is that every agriculturist in Tanjore is a hirer of labour or a hired man. No landowner here works for himself. Usually he prefers to give his land out for cultivation on *waram*, that is, share-cropping; or he employs landless labourers called *pannaiyals*—prior to 1948, they used to be hereditary farm employees and were little better than serfs who changed masters along with the transfer of land.

In the village of Agavamangudi, for example, there are 400 *mirasdars*. About ten per cent of them cultivate their land directly, which means through hired labour, while the remaining 90 per cent lease it out to tenants. Many tenants also do not work themselves. The pattern is repeated in every village.

Not that these "gentlemen" farmers are masters of extensive estates. In Agavamangudi, the 400 *mirasdars* own in all 600 acres of cultivated land, and only five or six of them possess as much as ten acres each. In the whole district of Tanjore, out of a total of 574,998 landowners, only 255 possess 100 acres or more; 504,620 have no

more than three acres; and of these, 401,742 *mirasdars* own one acre
and less. There is a three-tiered structure of rural society with the
landowner at the apex, under him the tenant and, finally, an army of
landless labourers at the base—in an area that has been under
ryotwari, that is, a system of peasant proprietorship, since 1804.

The gradations are clearly visible in the layout of the village. Solid
pillared mansions with tile floors owned by the big *mirasdars* stand
apart. Then there are the streets of medium-size brick houses with
tiled roofs belonging to the smaller landowners and non-working
tenants; and the entirely separate colonies of one-room huts with
mud walls and thatched roofs occupied by the labourer-cultivators
who also invariably happen to be *Harïans*, or members of other backward communities.

Not only has the system resulted in acute landlord-tenant tensions,
which compelled the Government of Madras recently to enact special
rent-regulating legislation for just this district[1] twice in four years,
but it seems also to have made both the landowner and the tenant
astonishingly indifferent to higher production, though obviously both
would stand to gain by it.

Mirasdars blame the tenant and hold the rent legislation responsible for his indifference. As Swaminathan, a *mirasdar* owning five
acres of land, put it: "Previously the tenant was getting 25 per cent
of the gross produce. Then Rajaji[2] increased his share to 40. Now
he is getting 60 per cent. So, naturally, he is more than satisfied and is
not interested in producing more. If we offer to give him five bags
of manure he says he wants only two. If we compel him to use more
fertilizer he objects because he has to pay for it. He is not interested
in our investing more either, because it adds to his costs."

Another landowner, Venkataraman, goes to the extent of sug-
gesting that "unless there is compulsion, production will not increase". It is his experience also that "if we give three bags of fertilizer to the tenant, he sells two and uses only one". Mohammed
Kassim owns only one acre, which he has duly leased out to a tenant.
The total yield from it is 15 bags[3] of paddy per annum of which
"I get only 40 per cent". He complains that while it is not sufficient
to maintain him at his middle-class standards, the tenant finds his

---

[1] "The Tanjore Tenants and Pannaiyal Protection Act, 1952." This was
amended in 1956 by "The Madras Cultivating Tenants (Payment of Fair Rent)
Act."

[2] C. Rajagopalachari, ex-Chief Minister of the State.

[3] One bag = 126 lbs.

share sufficient and is not interested in producing more, "because
thanks to the law he is now getting unexpected extra income."
"Also, since he cannot be evicted now, he feels very secure and com-
placent", adds another sufferer.

According to many tenants, however, it is the landowners who do
not take any interest in increasing production: "Although it is the
mirasdar's duty and responsibility to repair and desilt irrigation
channels, we have to do it free of cost. They are not doing it. Even
if they take two-thirds of the produce, they show no interest.[1] They
come one week before harvest, make an assessment and demand their
share. Many *mirasdars* do not even know the location of their fields."

Some tenants, however, frankly admit that they are not interested
in producing more. Thus another Swaminathan, a tenant who cultivates two acres on lease and gets 12 bags of paddy per annum as
his share, says he is quite satisfied. "If I produce more, the landlord
will ask for more." Similarly, Dakshinamoorthi is also a tenant of
one acre. He keeps 12 out of the 20 bags of paddy produced in the
year. There are six members in his family. He is quite positive:
"I don't need any more. It is more than enough."

Techniques and tools of cultivation in Tanjore also remain predominantly traditional despite the efforts of the State extension services and the presence of a modern government agricultural farm and
research station within the district. According to a recent Survey
Report, the government farm stands "as an isolated instance of improved agricultural practices amidst a wide zone which retains its old
uneconomic and rather inefficient practices".[2]

Why should it be so?

The obvious explanation—local opinion is unanimous on this—
would seem to lie in the fact that nature is so generous in this deltaic
region that it is unnecessary for people to exert much effort in order
to subsist. Hard work is not necessary. According to an agricultural
demonstrator in the district, whose work brings him in close touch
with the peasantry: "Even in a famine, the cultivator here does not
lose anything from his pocket. He could improve his output considerably in exactly the same set of circumstances, if only he would

---

[1] According to the law, a landlord is entitled to 40 per cent of the produce only.
In practice, however, he often takes as much as 60 per cent, or even more.

[2] *Pilot Survey of the Influence of the Mettur Irrigation and Hydro-Electric Project
on Agriculture and Agro-Industries in Pattukottai Taluk of the Tanjore District*, conducted under the auspices of the Planning Commission Research Programmes
Committee, Govt. of India, New Delhi, p. 81.

work more. But he doesn't. He is lazy. This is the general problem here and it is peculiar to Tanjore. In the districts of Salem and Coimbatore[1] the peasants are much more hard working because the soil there is dry and rocky and life is more difficult."

Yet, the above explanation cannot be the whole truth. For though admittedly Tanjore's is a paddy-rich society, the supposedly corroding prosperity is a pure myth in the case of the vast majority of its peasantry. The district has a strict mono-economy of rice culture, and it supports a rural population of nearly 2.5 million people on a cultivated area of 1,564,100 acres. Unlike his counterpart in most other areas, perhaps, even the poorest labourer in Tanjore eats rice, a much sought-after cereal, daily. But one meal in the morning of plain cold rice left over from the previous evening, and one meal in the evening of boiled rice again with a little curry, and occasionally some dried fish constitutes almost his entire diet. It is the end of his share in the general opulence. The majority have very little else, and they maintain themselves at a most primitive and minimal level.

In the *Harijan* colony of the village of Kabistalam, for example, they are all landless but like everyone else in this district are engaged in rice culture. In fact they are the primary producers, being the ultimate "hired" who actually work in the fields—gaunt faces, thin black bodies, all shirtless, their children with matted hair, in scanty rags or completely naked; in the background, mud walls under straw roofs and dark interiors with little in them beside a few pieces of unglazed pottery. Could they conceivably find life so comfortable that they do not want more?[2]

"If the government were to offer to give you as much land as you want, absolutely free of any charge, how much would you ask for?" I ask them. I repeat and clearly explain the magnanimous offer.

"You would like to have land of your own, wouldn't you?"

"Yes." Many heads nod.

"Then how much?"

---

[1] Also in Madras State.

[2] The average daily wage for agricultural labour in Madras State is 15·5 annas for men and 9·5 annas for women. Wage-paid employment averages only 178 days in the year, while the average annual income of a family is Rs.365—less than in any other State except Orissa. Madras also has the highest percentage of agricultural labour families in India. They constitute 53 per cent of its rural population. (These statistics pertain to Madras State as it was in 1951, before its reorganization into a smaller unit in 1956. They are based on *Census of India, 1951, and Reports of the All-India 1950–51 Agricultural Labour Enquiry*.)

Samu is the first to speak. He is an old man. He has never possessed any land. There are five members in his family. But he wants only one and one-third acres. He is precise. Even from that, he says after some mental calculation, he would be prepared to share 50 per cent of the produce with the *mirasdar*. Rangarajan is middle-aged, tall and slim. He also has five in his family to feed, and two acres would suffice. Manickam, with six in the family, already has three acres on lease. If he could, he would like to add to it two more acres. Srinivasan looks an artist. He wears a beard and shoulder-length hair. No, he is a mere labourer, has four in the family, wants just two acres and is prepared to share the produce on 50/50 basis. Vadival is a young man, clean shaven, one eye defective. I look to him more hopefully. But no, he also wants only two acres on a 60/40 basis. Govindan is already the proud cultivator of .03 acre which he has on lease. He has six in the family, wants only two acres and will be prepared to give 40 per cent of the produce to the landlord. Ammavin also is a young man, clean shaven and wearing a comparatively white *dhoti*. He has six in the family. With obvious hesitation he makes bold to ask for three acres, the produce of which he is prepared to share on 60/40 basis. And finally, it is the same story with another young hopeful—Velayuthan. There are nine in the family, and at present they are cultivating .3 acre. Yet he asks for only three acres on 60/40 basis.

"Are you sure you would not like to have more?" I ask again incredulously.

Yes, they are sure, quite sure.

The sun is setting on a roseate rice-girdled horizon. Mental horizons are apparently similarly circumscribed. Five acres on lease is the limit of their aspiration. Only Manickam wants so much. Their demands are calculated solely on the basis of the family's consumption requirements of rice at two meals a day, one of which is cold and left over from the previous night. For the time being at least, they do not want more.

The CMP

Rice in these parts is not relished merely for its taste. It also carries status. It is the food of the well-to-do classes, who take it daily for all their meals throughout the year. On the other hand, the poor, except in areas like Tanjore, even if they have only one meal a day, can afford only a cheaper millet, such as *ragi* or *cumbu*. For unless they themselves cultivate paddy it lies beyond their reach. They cannot afford to purchase it since of all the cereals available it is the most expensive. Therefore, if a man can grow paddy on his own little plot or even if it be on leased land, he is supremely happy. He will not generally take it to the market and sell it to buy a cheaper grain for consumption and so make a profit. He will eat it and sell only the surplus, if any.

So when I enquire in Sangamangalam: "What would you say has made the greatest difference in your lives in the past ten years", the reply is unanimous—just the one word *CMP*. These three English letters have passed into the local Tamil dialect.

"The CMP! but that was nearly thirty years ago", I protest.

They are seated on the floor—unshaven chins, an occasional shirt, puzzled eyes. There is silence. How about the Five Year Plan, I suggest. Yes, some of them did hear of it at the time of the general election, a year ago. On the wall opposite is still pasted a large poster inscribed "How Should You Vote"—the caption in English. Candidates of various political parties had come then and mentioned something about a Plan, they say, though some among them do not remember. Many do not know that a Plan exists. None, however, is clear as to what it is. Nor has it in any manner touched them or their village. No, they are unable to think of anything except the CMP.

It is the same story at Padapanavayal, about eight miles away. Both the villages lie in the Pattukottai *taluk*[1] of the district of Tanjore. CMP stands for the Cauvery Mettur Project which was constructed in 1934 and which, while improving the existing irrigation facilities in the rest of the district, extended them for the first time to Pattukottai, till then a dry area.

These villages, therefore, received canal water irrigation for the first time with the construction of the CMP. As a result, acreage under paddy in Pattukottai *taluk* increased from 57,748 acres in 1931 to 179,500 acres in 1951, and it transformed the region's entire pattern of cropping and consumption. The peasants here also could cultivate paddy extensively, and though they may not yet have a shirt to wear they do eat rice. They have not forgotten that they owe it to the CMP.

[1] Within a State in India, *district* is normally the basic unit of all civil administration. A district is further sub-divided into a number of revenue circles called *taluks*.

Stolen Waters

This obsession for rice is perhaps one reason why irrigation waters never run unused for a day in Madras, as they do in many other areas where there is often a considerable time lag between the completion of an irrigation work and its full utilization. No extraneous persuasion is required in this State to induce a peasant to change over from dry to wet cultivation, because wet cultivation here means paddy.

Thus in Villarasampatty, a village in Coimbatore district,[1] I enquire of another peasant, Rakkiagounder: "Tell me, what difference do you find in life now as compared to 40 years ago?"

He is a grand old man of 70 odd years, his thin face deeply lined, with a moustache, still some black hair, shirtless, a towel over one shoulder. His reply is unhesitating and direct:

"Forty years ago I was getting a yield of four bags of *bajra* per acre. Now also I am getting the same. Forty years ago I was getting my food, and I am getting it now. But, whereas 40 years ago I was eating mainly *ragi*, now I am eating rice."

It is because three of his 19 acres have come under irrigation recently, and he is growing paddy on them.

"But is that all—the only difference you notice?" I ask again. "Surely the world has changed much in 40 years in many other respects."

He is positive. Yes, that is all, except that "prices of goods and labour are forever rising higher and higher". As an afterthought, he adds casually one more item: that his three sons did not go to school but his grand-children are doing so now.

Unlike Tanjore, however, cultivation of paddy on a large scale is a recent innovation in the district of Coimbatore, and this again is due to another irrigation project, one of the first and the biggest to be completed in Madras State after independence.[2] It is called the Lower Bhavani Project—LBP for short. The Bhavani is a tributary of the same river Cauvery which irrigates Tanjore. And here too the LBP overshadows everything else. Its waters were used as rapidly as they could reach the channels, and the cry now is for more water, which the project is unable to supply. That is because, unlike the CMP, the Lower Bhavani was not designed to convert dry lands into paddy lands, but simply to provide an assured water supply for "dry"

[1] Another district within the same State of Madras.
[2] Work on the project was started in 1949 and completed in 1956.

C

crops such as millets and cotton, which were already under cultivation, and which require watering only once in five or ten days. Coimbatore is predominantly a millet growing area. Only the seepage areas along the LBP canals have been earmarked for paddy, a mere 10,000 out of a total of 207,000 acres which the Project is meant to irrigate ultimately. Otherwise, its cultivation is specifically prohibited.

The peasants, however, want to cultivate paddy, and practically every farmer whose land has received irrigation is doing so, despite the government's order, by drawing more water than is legally permitted. In 1957–58, approximately 44,000 acres, as against the 10,000 permitted, were already under rice, and many peasants were paying a penalty of as much as Rs.60 an acre for doing so.

A typical example is Parameswaram of Kalingiam, who owns ten acres of land. Previously he could cultivate rice only in 25 cents[1] which were irrigated from a well he shared with his neighbour. Now he is growing paddy in seven acres. As a consequence, in 1956, when he first received the canal waters, he says he paid a penalty of Rs.180; in 1957 of Rs.200; in 1958 he has been fined Rs.300.[2] Even so, he continues to cultivate rice. "Merchants come to me and purchase it", he says proudly.

In the *taluk* of Gobi, where this village is situated, the penalties imposed for this year alone amount to about Rs.350,000 for illegal cultivation of rice on the LBP irrigated lands.[3] The cultivators have been fined three or four times already—fines ranging from Rs.15 to Rs.60 an acre. Still they persist. What is even more strange is that paddy is replacing not only millets but in many instances commercial crops of greater value than rice, such as tobacco, chilli and cotton!

---

[1] One cent is a hundredth part of an acre.

[2] The figures include the water rates.

[3] Besides paddy, peasants in Coimbatore are also cultivating a second irrigated crop on 50,000 acres, although *no* second crop was contemplated under the Bhavani scheme.

KERALA

CHAPTER II

POVERTY AMIDST PLENTY

LEGEND has it that the Hindu sage Parasurama reclaimed the land now called Kerala from the ocean in order to settle 64 families of *Namboodri Brahmins*. The same area—15,000 square miles, of which only one-third is arable—holds today more than 16 million people. It is the smallest and the most densely populated State in India, a narrow belt on the southern tip of the west coast, 340 miles long and never more than 70 miles in width. A ridge of mountains descends gently to a palm-fringed beach. The higher country is covered with lush forests where wild elephants roam and studded with neat plantations of tea and rubber. Winding valleys below are rippling rivers of paddy. The entire landscape is always green and sparkling with lakes, lagoons, streams and navigable backwaters.

It is about 35 miles across the border by Cochin Express from Coimbatore in Madras to Olavakot in Palaghat district of Kerala, but nowhere have I seen such a small distance make so striking a difference. And the difference is not merely scenic with minor variations in the cultural overtones, as normally occur within different linguistic groups in a particular zone anywhere in India.

The language, of course, changes from the Tamil of Madras to Malayalam. But whereas male apparel is nearly the same, the female dress is completely different. Instead of the usual sari women here wear a simple sarong with a blouse—as in distant Ceylon and eastern India, in Assam and Manipur. The silks of Conjeevaram give way to plain cotton, and instead of brilliant purples, reds and orange, white predominates and it is usually washed and sparkling.

There is much less nakedness. Men do not, as in Madras, work in the fields with only a square piece of cloth in front; nor is a morning drive in the countryside blemished by the sight of a row of squatting backs. Instead, one encounters a continuous stream of neatly-dressed

children on their way to school, bags bulging with books. The
temple structure and the atmosphere within is also different, though
the gods are the same.

The village itself is radically different in Kerala. The State has a
large rural population, but it is not divided into self-contained and
segregated village groups with some identity of interests and outlook and a distinctive appearance, as in most of the other parts of
India. Here, habitation is continuous, and each little house, whether
urban or rural, stands independently, its backyard a patchwork
plantation of a little of everything—tapioca, jackfruit, arecanut, coconut, pepper, vegetables, and a bush or two of red hibiscus in the
hedge for colour. In fact, it is difficult to tell where a town ends and
a village begins and whereas in Madras and elsewhere, the smallest
village is a miniature slum, in Kerala even industrial towns do not
have slums.

Alwaye, for example, is a town in Ernakulam district. Because it
was one of the earliest to get cheap power and it is situated on the
banks of a navigable river, many of the State's biggest industries,
both government-owned and private, are concentrated here.

"Please take me to your slums. I want to meet the factory
workers," I requested. There was consternation all round.

"But we have no slums in the sense you mean", I was informed.
"The labour is mainly local and it is scattered. Workers live in their
own houses, five, six, eight, even ten miles away. It would be very
difficult to find them."

Here, I was further told, even some of the largest industrial estab-
lishments do not provide special accommodation for their workmen
in what are known as labour colonies, as is customary in other parts
of the country. There are single-storied tin-roofed "lines" in the
tea estates in the upper regions in Kerala but they are used almost
entirely by imported Tamil labour. Malayalees[1] do not work in tea
gardens.

There is the Indian Aluminium Company in Alwaye. It has built
quarters for its workmen, but only twenty, though its total labour
strength is nearly a thousand. The houses are compact and attractive
and have more space than the usual standard provided for in such
industrial housing schemes. They have a verandah, two rooms,
kitchen, bathroom, another verandah at the back and a separate
washroom. The rooms are well ventilated, and there is electricity

[1] Natives of Kerala are known as Malayalees.

and running water. But to fill even these 20 houses the Company's management has had to beg families to occupy them, and some of those who obliged want to leave now. One of the quarters is still lying vacant; it was never occupied. The workers prefer, it seems, to live in their own homes, even if they be one-room palm-leaf cottages. The Company has suspended its housing programme, therefore, and the large area acquired by it for the purpose is lying vacant.

A Typical Industrial Worker

Kumaran is a worker at Indian Aluminium. He lives far out in Ernakulam in a wooden L-shaped cabin with two very small and dark rooms and a thatched roof. It has no electricity or running water.

Yes, Kumaran does find life better than it was ten years ago. Then he was earning only two rupees a day. Now he gets five. He is able to afford better food despite the high prices; in those earlier days he remembers he often went hungry. He has been working for 18 years now. Slim and tall, he looks young however. There are a few books on a small table, two chairs and a bench along the wall, and a small timepiece in a wooden box. In the inner room clothes hang on a line; there is a double bed and two small trunks. No, he has not been able to save anything apart from the Provident Fund. That is still intact. He has a wife and three children. The youngest less than a year old, is sleeping on a mat on the floor. The other two have gone to school. Five others are dead.

Kumaran spends six rupees a month on the bus fare in going to the factory, which is about ten miles away, but says that he does not mind the expense nor the distance. He would not like to shift and live in the accommodation provided by the Company.

"No, I would not mind paying the ten rupees in rent", he says, "but there is no privacy in the factory quarters."

He is keen on privacy and the factory houses are built four to a block. Here he has a neat little compound—two and a half cents of land—where his cow is tethered, and the setting is essentially rural. Though the residents in the locality are mostly fishermen, backward and poor, the whole colony is in the midst of a coconut grove, and each house or hut, however small, is in a separate yard, almost every one of which is remarkably clean.

Marx and Aerodromes

The rural population of Kerala, on the other hand, is highly urban in character. Its women enjoy remarkable freedom and hold an important position in the family, while people in the villages in this State have an outlook and set of values which are in many respects different from those of their counterparts in most parts of India. Though rice is the staple food in Kerala also, the peasants' horizons are generally not limited to paddy alone, as in Tanjore or Coimbatore.

In fact, few farmers here appear to find paddy an attractive or a paying proposition. At a three-day camp at Mankara there are 50 of them from four neighbouring villages under training to be "village leaders". None of them are landless labourers, but neither are there any big landlords. Most of them are small owner-cultivators or tenants. Their lands are not irrigated. Even so, many of them are growing two crops of paddy. Not a single person in the group, however, admits that he is making a profit, and those who have been educated up to High School standard are trying their best to get out of agriculture and seek a salaried job. In general, they are smart, clean shaven and neatly dressed in shirts and clean white *lungis*. The younger ones among them look more like University students than agriculturists. Small of build, there is nothing muscular or rustic about them. On the contrary, they look very middle class. Many wear wrist watches. Some of them speak fluent English.

In a village audience here it would be naïve to enquire: "Have you heard of the Five Year Plan?" On the other hand, you may be called upon to discuss Marx, or to explain "why the government of India discriminates against Kerala and makes such small allocations for development expenditure" or "what the government proposes to do about the acute unemployment situation in the State".

When Bhaskara Menon took over as Block Development Officer of a National Extension Service Block in Chittur and called his first meeting of the local people to ask them, in true textbook extension style to let him know their most urgent "felt need," the reply was: "We want an aerodrome". Menon was stumped, since the National Extension Services' schematic budget as devised in distant New Delhi provides at most for dry-weather village approach roads barely usable by bullock carts; it has no provision for aerodromes. But the incident is typical of Kerala.

Actually, barring a small portion in the north which was part of

Madras till 1956, in no other State are the rural areas so extensively developed. Here, for example, there is a network of excellent
roads and power is the cheapest in India; most of the villages have
electricity. Medical services are good, and in the field of social education there is no need to run a campaign on the benefits of soap because
the people are already accustomed to bathing twice a day. Some dirt
and personal untidiness are to be found only in the lowest strata
among the *Harijans*. Kerala has more children—90 per cent—in
school than any other State in the country. There is a school within
walking distance of almost every child, though they are mostly
private. Similarly, adult literacy is widespread: 75 per cent of the
men and 55 per cent of the women are literate as against the 18 per
cent average for the whole of India. Many a street sweeper, even,
reads a newspaper before he goes to work. One small district like
Kottayam has five dailies. The library movement here is perhaps the
most widespread in the country. Almost every village has a genuine
library with anything from 1,000 to 4,000 books and several hundred
members.

In raw materials also the State is extremely rich. It has mineral
deposits of ilmenite, silimanite, granite, and the only deposits in India
of thorium-bearing monazite sands. It has excellent china clay and
white sands suitable for glass making. Its forests produce valuable
timbers, such as teak, sandalwood, blackwood and rose wood. Some
of these are said to have been taken to build King Solomon's palace,
for so long have they been famous. Bamboo is in abundance, and
there are several minor forest products of commercial value, such as
honey, lac, cloves, wax, cane, ivory, medicinal herbs, and so on.

Besides, Kerala has a three-hundred-mile coastline with enormous
fishing resources, and though the State is deficient in paddy there are
a number of valuable commercial crops which bring in much more
money. These are cardamom, ginger, jack fruit, cashew nuts, lemon
grass, rubber, coconut and coir, tapioca, arecanut, tea, and, of course,
pepper, the "black gold" for which Vasco da Gama hazarded the
historic voyage around the stormy Cape of Good Hope to reach
Calicut on 20th May in 1498. The soil is fertile, and every inch of
arable land is cultivated. Indeed, it would be difficult to imagine—
in the Indian context—a strip of territory more richly endowed, both
with material and human resources.

There is, however, also the high pressure of population, low productivity, wasteful under-exploitation of available resources, and

above all, a serious lack of enterprise. For example, when the State government built a number of "industrial estates" under its Second Five Year Plan to encourage the growth of small and medium industries to relieve unemployment, a sufficient number of people could not be found within Kerala to come forward and avail themselves of the scheme, even though the government offered to provide not only the premises and power, but also the necessary machinery on hire-purchase, working capital on easy credit, as well as training facilities, a marketing organization, and in some cases the promise to purchase the entire output. An average Malayalee, it would appear, would prefer the security of a small job than take any risk whatever.

In spite of the plentiful resources and the presence of so many of the conventional pre-requisites of development, therefore, the citizen of Kerala has a per capita income of Rs.217.9.[1] It is about the lowest in the country; the budget of the State is always in deficit; its rural population is 84 per cent of the State's total; and the unemployment figures, for the educated and for agricultural labour, are among the highest in India.[2] The State continues to be afflicted by all the basic ills and problems of under-development that plague the rest of the sub-continent.

---

[1] In 1955–56. The all-India figure for the same year was Rs.260·6.

[2] Both in wages and employment days, however, the agricultural labourer in Kerala (of 1951–52) is better off than his counterpart in Madras. His wage rate is 21·4 annas per day and employment average 215 days in the year, as against 15·5 annas and 178 days in Madras. It is interesting to note that the wage rate is higher in Kerala, even though it shares with Madras the honour of having the highest incidence of unemployment among its agricultural labour. Average annual income of an agricultural labour family in Kerala is Rs.541 as against Rs.365 in Madras. (Figures based on *Census of India 1951* and *Reports of the All-India Agricultural Labour Enquiry, 1950–51*).

CHAPTER III

LANDLORDS AND THE LANDLESS

WALYAR is a small irrigation project in northern Kerala. There is a lake, with a dam to one side and hills to the other. The sky to the west is a blaze of colour, with the mountains below it in a veil of mist, a delicate mauve edged with gold.

Here I met Narayanamurthi, a landlord who has nearly 2,000 acres of land, of which he himself cultivates only 80 through hired labour, even though the yield on that is 130 *paras*[1] per acre per crop, while the yield to the tenants to whom he has leased out the rest of the land seldom exceeds 80 *paras*. The tenants pay him 70 *paras* per acre as rent from the two crops they grow in a year.

Narayanamurthi feels that with the fixing of a minimum wage for agricultural labour[2] and other land reforms of recent years tensions between labour and employer are on the increase. It is not bad in these parts yet, he says, because this, the Malabar area as a whole, is more backward than the rest. "Even so, relations are not as cordial as before, though in my case nobody has gone to court."

He has had no trouble with his labourers, he thinks, because he gives his permanent employees work all the year round. He also gives them loans when they need them. Then, on the occasion of two festivals in the year, he gives them clothes and a gift of one *para* of paddy per head. When there is a birth in the family, he gives one *para* of grain if it is a male child and a half-*para* if it is a female.

"That is because the male child will work for me when he grows up. It is the convention, The girl will go away after marriage. Yes, it is a long-term policy and I am still following it. There is nothing to prevent a man from leaving if he wants to, but he must work for

---

[1] One *para* = 16¾ lbs.

[2] For ordinary agricultural operations it is fixed at Rs.1·50 for men and Rs.1·00 for women per day.

at least one year if I give him one *para* of rice on the day of *Onam*[1] and he accepts it. It becomes an oral contract.

"My labourers are still working for me as before, on the same terms. They did ask for more. So I gave them the minimum wage but withdrew the other facilities—clothes, loans, and gifts on births, deaths and festivals. Then they came back to me of their own accord and told me and the local revenue official that they wanted to continue the old system." This is, it seems, a fairly common occurrence.

"I have 40 such permanent labourers—20 male and 20 female", adds Narayanamurthi. "I am prepared to give them work for all the 365 days, but they do not come every day. They are irregular, either because they feel like having a rest or because they are just lazy. They are all *Harijans*. I have given them free land on which they make their own huts. They are not paid for the days they are absent."

He himself does no work; he only supervises. He uses no mechanized methods of cultivation.

Portrait of Another Landlord

In the district of Trichur we meet another landlord, one of the biggest in Kerala. We drive through a huge estate to reach the house, a solid double-storied structure. Everything around as far as the eye can see is his.

I am taken to an upper room—it is a long hall—by a narrow wooden staircase. The room itself is packed like an auction mart with furniture and chairs of every description—divans of various designs, easy chairs, straight-backed chairs, and so on. Every one of these is upholstered in a different colour, mostly worn out and faded, and the one I sit on is in light green satin with pink frills. On the walls hang many painted portraits, presumably of members of the family, wall calendars of the current as well as of a number of past years, group photographs, mounted bison horns, and several mirrors.

The host himself is extremely interesting. With grey hair close clipped, he sits without a shirt in his white muslin *dhoti*, in which is tucked a bunch of keys. He wears no shoes, as no one in Kerala ever does inside his house. His forehead, arms and chest are covered with lines of sandalwood paste, and he wears the sacred thread. He has a full set of very white teeth—I am unable to make out whether they are real or false—and he takes snuff every now and then. His skin is light and smooth.

[1] An important harvest festival in Kerala.

When he speaks, he uses not only both his hands to the tips of his tapering fingers, but eyes, eyebrows, facial muscles and the shoulders. It is a symphony in movement, and, as in a Kathakali dance, the ripples go right down to his waist, which is still very slim. Even though he is speaking on so mundane a subject as land reform, the intonation is musical; one can beat time as he talks. He does not speak or understand English.

His reaction to land reforms—proposed imposition of a ceiling on land holdings and the fixing of a minimum wage for agricultural labour—is perfectly logical and natural. He feels that they will affect the landlords adversely. And, of course, all this encouragement being given to labour is absolutely disastrous. "The *Harijans* to whom I gave small housing sites to guard my coconut trees, you know, now they have begun to steal my coconuts, and I dare not do anything about it."

On most of his lands he is practising direct cultivation by employing labourers. But off-hand he cannot remember how much land he has. His secretary, another shirtless man, also plastered with sandalwood paste, brings out a register, sits on the floor to study it and takes a long time to find out. After many calculations, totallings and several corrections, it finally emerges that his holding is over 2,100 acres of which 1,200 acres is under paddy. The rest is in coconut groves. The per capita holding in the State of Kerala as a whole is 0.3 acres. In this particular area the average farm size is one to one and a half acres.

Our landlord is positive and emphatic that, if a ceiling is imposed on land holdings, agricultural production will deteriorate and the output of food will go down. "So-called cultivators with only 15 acres of land[1] will have neither the interest nor the capacity to make the necessary investment to produce more."

"But are you producing more than the average in this region?"

No, he is not. He harvests more than 70,000 *paras* of paddy every year, but his yields are only 80 *paras* in an acre, which is poor. He is conscious of the fact that he is not using sufficient quantities of fertilizer in the scientific manner. But "if I do that then the margin of profit will decrease". In his calculation that is the decisive factor against improving his technique of cultivation. He has not tried the Japanese method of paddy cultivation either, because "it is not

[1] This was the proposed ceiling on double-crop land in the then "Kerala Agrarian Relations Bill, 1957."

the fashion here", and he is convinced that the result will not be commensurate with the investment and effort, because some of his friends have tried.[1]

The Coolies

Between Aleppey and Vembanad Lake is a small island in an area which is served entirely by waterways, an idyllic scene with the banks lined thickly with a fringe of coconut trees, little thatched cottages on narrow strips of land, boats plying to and fro, all reflected in the water. The foot-path is broad enough only for walking in single file. Paddy fields are flooded. It is one of the richest rice-growing areas.

This is the house of a landless labourer, a coolie as he is called. It has no estate around it, and the land on which it stands belongs to another. It is single-storied and made entirely of dry coconut leaves sewn together with coconut fibre. The door is low and leads into one very small room. It has no chairs, divans, or even a bed. There is only a small *chula*—but no ash in it. Some tattered clothes lie in a heap in one corner, like a mangy dog asleep.

The man has gone out to look for work. The woman is at home. She also works whenever she can find any work. Five children, almost naked, stand around with big hungry eyes.

"We manage somehow to eat one meal a day, all the year round. We can never be sure of the second meal and usually we have to do without it." They are always paid in kind—she never handles money. She looks old, perhaps prematurely, and faded like the upholstery on the chairs of the Trichur landlord. As she speaks her eyes are wet.

Near by stands another woman. Chirutha is her name. Her attitude is fidgety, uncertain, purposeless. She must be between 40 and 50, she says. "How can I remember?" She has only a black thread round her throat and no bangles, because she is a widow. She has a daughter and a small son living with her.

Her hair, still black, is drawn back tight and tied in a small knot. One strand has escaped to fall over the right cheek. The face is thin and oval; with wrinkles near the eyes; a little nose turned up at the end gives it a pert touch. Small of build and frail, she could have

---

[1] This line of argument prevails very widely among rice cultivators in Madras and in Kerala, and in most parts of India, in fact, both among landowners and tenants, big and small. The increase in gross output and therefore income does not interest them if the margin of profit per para or bag of rice decreases thereby, which it normally does of course, with heavier investments in fertilizer and labour such as the Japanese method or any more scientific method of cultivation must involve.

been pretty when young. But now the teeth are stained and the lips chapped and dry, and so are the breasts—like sucked mangoes. She clutches a small, dirty rag to them with both hands, for she wears only a frayed *lungi* from the waist down to just below the knees. Her slim back and shoulders are bare.

No, she does not live here but on a similar island near by. She came in search of work. This season she has been able to get some employment, but none for the last two days. Today also she could not find anything to do.

The measure of paddy that Chirutha last earned in wages "will finish tonight after we have had our supper. There will be none for tomorrow."

MYSORE

CHAPTER IV

POVERTY'S MILLIONAIRES

IT is a natural assumption, made mainly by those who have never known real poverty, that a poor man can never be in doubt about his problems. He does not have enough for what economists would define as his "absolute" needs, such as food, clothing and housing, and therefore he must want more.[1] Depending on one's philosophy of life, it is said, one may or may not be inclined to exert oneself for luxuries. Beyond a certain stage of affluence one may not even be clear as to precisely what one needs. But it should not be necessary to tell a hungry man that he requires food and that he must work to obtain it.

Yet Balappa, a landless agricultural labourer in Gangawati *taluk* of the State of Mysore, has returned from work though the time is only noon. He was fortunate to get work today. But now he is reclining against the wall of his hut smoking a *bidi*.

"How is it you are back so early? Are you not going to work for the rest of the day?"

"No", is the brief reply.

"Why?"

"I am tired."

He is a young man; has a wife and a child and one cow.

"How much have you been paid for half a day's work?"

"One and a half *seers* of *jowar*."

"But are you able to get work all the year round that you can afford to take it so easy?" I persist.

"No."

"Then what do you do when you have no work?"

"Sit at home and borrow and eat. What else can I do?"

"Why don't you work for the whole day when work is available

[1] See J. K. Galbraith, *The Affluent Society*, Hamish Hamilton, 1958, pp. 1, 2.

46

and save for lean times?" I ask again, unable to restrain myself from offering gratuitous advice.

"Oh, I have to get grass for my cow. If I work in the afternoon as well, when will I get the grass for the cow?", he says, throwing away the still smoking stump of the *bidi* with a gesture of dismissing the debate.

It is not food alone that Balappa lacks for many days in the year. His clothes are torn and dirty, and his house is a small one-room mud hut with a thatch which his family shares with the cow. But he relaxes by the time it is noon and, of his own choice, does not go back to work even when it is available. He possesses nothing but poverty; yet a millionaire could not care less.

They Do Not Want More

Gangawati is in the district of Raichur and it has had the good fortune of being irrigated recently by the Tungabhadra project. A major irrigation and hydro-electric scheme of South India, its irrigation waters were let out for the first time in July 1953.

The project is located in Mysore near Hospet and commands a total area of two million acres stretching across into the neighbouring State of Andhra as well, in a belt which has been notorious for centuries for recurring droughts and famines. Its 127-mile long Left Bank Canal, however, is designed to irrigate Mysore territory only, in the single district of Raichur. Like the Lower Bhavani Project, Tungabhadra also is meant primarily for "light irrigation" of dry crops such as *jowar*, groundnut, and cotton, which are already under extensive cultivation in this region.[1] In Raichur, *jowar* is the principal cereal crop and also the staple food.

But whereas in Coimbatore the Bhavani waters were taken up as soon as they could reach the fields and there is a clamour for more, in Balappa's village not one single peasant has yet deigned to avail himself of the irrigation facilities from the Tungabhadra. This, even though for the first three years the water is being offered free of any charge.

Meerappa also belongs to this village. Two of his front teeth are missing. He wears a white shirt, *dhoti* and turban. He owns ten acres of land. The irrigation channel passes right through his property. But he lets the water flow by unused.

[1] Out of 570,332 acres covered by the Left Bank Canal, 490,322 acres are earmarked for "light irrigation" only.

"It rained last year so I did not take. It has rained this year also, so I have not taken. I will take when the rains fail", he concedes, grudgingly, but not very convincingly, because even this year the rains were not regular.

"Have you made the field channels at least?"

"No."

According to an official of the project: "We carry manures and improved seeds in a trailer and offer to deliver them right at the doorstep to induce these cultivators to use them. We offer them loans to buy the seeds and manures. We go to their fields and offer to let in the water for them. We request them to try it out first in two acres only if they are not convinced. They could quadruple their yields if they would only take our advice and at least experiment. Still they are not coming forward."

To date, out of 41,000 acres for which water has been made available in this *taluk* for "light irrigation," only 3,000 acres or so have been actually irrigated and that too, "only this year, because the rains were not timely".

Cheerful Optimists

"That is true", confirms Theemappa in another village in the same district. "Everyone who comes here, from the *Gram Sewak*[1] upward, tells us to irrigate our crops. High officials come and say the same thing."

Theemappa has 48 acres of land which are irrigable. Another peasant, Timman Gowda has 40 acres, of which 20 are irrigable. Ishwar Gowda has a farm of 60 acres. They and several others have been taken to the government farm at Gangawati and shown how, owing to the use of fertilizer with irrigation, *jowar* stands over six feet with grain heads at least three times as big as their own miserable specimen. It is there now for all to see, ready for the sickle, and it will yield 2,200 to 3,000 lbs. an acre as against their own average yield of one or two, or at the most three bags—one bag being equal to 164 lbs. They admit they have seen the *jowar* at the government farm and that they know they can increase their own yields. Even so, Ishwar Gowda has not taken the canal water; nor has Theemappa or Timman Gowda. In the course of the last two years, in fact, that water has been available in this village, only three of its 100 culti-

---

[1] *Gram Sewak* is the Village Level Worker (VLW for short) in the Community Development Organization.

1. A woman Social Education Organiser of the Community Development Organisation teaching the little children in the Harijan section of a village in Madras State. (Chapter I.)

2. The Lower Bhavani Dam, one of the first and the biggest irrigation projects to be completed in Madras State after independence. (Chapter I.)

3. Demonstration of the Japanese method of transplantation of paddy seedlings by the Young Farmer's Club of a Girls' High School, in Kerala. (Chapters II & III.)

4. A new well constructed in a village in Mysore under the Community Development scheme. (Chapter IV.)

vators could be persuaded so far to irrigate seven out of the 535 acres that have been made irrigable.

And so it is that in this proverbially parched and thirsty land another crop of *jowar* is under harvest and women sit by the roadside tying the sheaves to load the bullock carts. Yet the area actually irrigated lags far behind the area that has been made irrigable and more than two-thirds of the water continues to run waste.

"After all, we have been growing our crops like this with only rain water for thousands of years", is the normal reply, accompanied by a shrug of the shoulder. And then the rain is free, while for the canal water they will have to pay once they agree to take it, irrespective of whether they use it or not. The peasant here is obviously not interested in increasing his productivity, which irrigation makes possible, but looks upon the latter simply as insurance against drought. For irrigation by itself will not give the maximum increase in crop yields, but only a more scientific technique of cultivation combined with the use of fertilizer and irrigation.

By the present method, on the other hand, the *jowar* grows almost by itself. The farmer simply broadcasts the seed after superficial ploughing and then returns only to harvest it. It involves no investment such as the new method requires—of using fertilizers, doing inter-culture and letting in water at regular intervals. And since there is plenty of land here, even at the rate of one or two bags an acre, the yield is sufficient to feed the family and often to enable it to tide over an intervening year of drought as well.

That is not all. These peasants are such brave and cheerful optimists that, despite the many droughts and famines they have had to face so often, they have not even bothered to sink any wells. The Tungabhadra project is a recent gift. But through the centuries practically no wells have been made in this district to assist in farming. Well irrigation is negligible, confined to only about 2,000 acres out of a total cultivated area of 2,532,000 acres. Sub-soil water, they say, is too low—30 to 40 feet deep and brackish.

In Coimbatore also, conditions are similar.[1] The water level there is even lower, normally not less than 50 and often 100 feet or more,

---

[1] The comparison holds true for the two States of Mysore and Madras as well. Thus, at the end of the Second Plan period (1960–61), gross irrigation potential from continuing major and medium irrigation schemes in Madras is anticipated to cover 545,000 acres, and its utilization is expected to be 100 per cent. In Mysore, on the other hand, the potential will be 780,000 acres, but its utilization is anticipated to be for only 475,000 acres. (*Third Five Year Plan—A Draft Outline*, Planning Commission, Govt. of India, June 1960, p. 193).

D

while conditions of climate and crops cultivated are almost identical. Yet long before Bhavani Sagar was constructed, Coimbatore was covered with a network of irrigation wells, all on private initiative. In fact, whereas canals in Coimbatore, including those of the LBP, irrigate a total of 242,571 acres, wells in the district numbering 110,952 irrigate an area of 366,725 acres. Despite the sub-soil water being brackish there also, these wells have converted "dry" lands into "garden" lands and have enabled extensive cultivation of valuable commercial crops such as tobacco and chilli, as well as of the beloved paddy. In Raichur, on the other hand, even drinking water generally is not drawn from wells but from the numerous streams which cut across the terrain. When these dry up in summer, the villager simply scoops the water out of the stream bed by digging in a little.

Scarcity of Labour

Some observers of the Indian economy suggest that low levels of efficiency in India in any field of production can be ascribed to the abundance of labour and its appalling cheapness. To them, one key to India's rapid progress might lie in somehow making labour scarce. Then efficiency would increase automatically, they say, and people would learn to work themselves diligently and conscientiously to their maximum capacity. There would be less wastage and more production.

In Raichur, in this respect, conditions approximate to the ideal. Density of population is only 168 persons per square mile, and though on paper the average land holding works out to 15.4 acres—even that is high by Indian standards[1]—in actual fact many have 40 to 60 acres. Yet agricultural productivity here—there is no other kind—is extremely low. What is more, it is so according to both official and popular assessment, and development is not taking place rapidly enough, primarily because labour is allegedly scarce, though it is not at all expensive.[2]

"Where is the labour?" is a familiar cry in Raichur, and in fact, its scarcity is the main defence here of all backwardness—for not

[1] The all India average is 7·5 acres, while for Mysore as a whole it is 10·8 acres.

[2] In fact agricultural labour in Mysore is cheapest in the southern zone—the daily wage rate here being only 14·6 annas as against 15·5 annas in Madras, and 21·4 annas in Kerala. In Raichur, which was part of Hyderabad in 1950–51, to which period these statistics relate, agricultural wages were even lower, at 13·1 annas, in spite of the scarcity.

making drains or school buildings, some of which have been lying half-completed for three years, for not keeping the village streets clean, for not using fertilizers, for lands lying fallow, for not digging the field channels, for not irrigating, and so on. Even the landless, the labourers themselves, complain of it, as for example, Balappa, when he asked who would bring the grass for his cow if he went back to work. The local administration, therefore, is making every effort to reduce this scarcity by importing labour from other, more crowded, neighbourhoods.

CHAPTER V

LEISURED MEN AND WORKING WIVES

RAICHUR became a part of Mysore only recently, after the reorganization of the States in November 1956. Till then it was part of old Hyderabad, a most backward tract in a backward kingdom.

Mysore, on the other hand, was well developed by 1947. Like Hyderabad it was an autonomous unit under its own ruler in British times, but Mysore was fortunate to be served by a series of enlightened *Dewans* who gave it an administration in several respects superior to that anywhere else in India, so that it came to be known as a model State.

Thus, it was one of the earliest to enter the modern industrial age, to foster science and technology, and to provide irrigation and power and such amenities of modern life as good roads, schools and hospitals—though they did not extend to the rural areas to the same extent as in the States of Travancore and Cochin, which now constitute Kerala. The Bhadravati Iron and Steel Works were started by the Mysore Government as early in 1923, while the first hydroelectric plant in India was commissioned in this State in 1902 with an installed capacity of 5,130 kw.

Now, the State has several well-developed large, medium and cottage scale industries, surplus revenues, and plenty of natural resources, such as fertile soils, rich forests, a coastline, and a variety of minerals. Every pebble in Bellary is 67 per cent iron, while Kolar is the sole surviving supplier of gold in the whole of India. Mysore is also one of the few fortunate States to have a reasonably low density of population—only 259 persons per square mile as against more than 1,000 in Kerala—so that, barring small pockets, there is no undue pressure on the land.

The "Show Piece"

In the darkness, only a dull roar; as the first rays of dawn sweep into the landscape, a cascading mass of foam turns a pure gold, veiled in a delicate transparent cloud of spray. It has rained, and the Shimsha falls are muddy, full and heavy. Shimsha is a tributary of the river Cauvery, and the district of Mandya in southern Mysore, where these waterfalls are situated, is one of the State's most prosperous and highly developed regions—its "show piece".

Education is claimed to be popular here, and the district is extremely well served by roads which have been financed mainly from a local tax levied on sugar cane. Irrigation came here some 30 years back with the Visvesvarayya Channel. Paddy is the main crop, and a yield of 18 to 20 pallas[1] per acre is claimed to be an easy average. Unlike Raichur, where the family's wealth is normally buried in the ground in an earthen vessel, here all the more well-to-do houses in the village have an iron safe, and at least one double bed for furniture.

In the Malavalli taluk of this district was set up in 1952, in collaboration with the Ford Foundation, a Pilot Project for Community Development, and it was fortunate to have the assistance of a couple of devoted officers whose names have become household legend for their excellent extension work in agriculture. The result, according to official statistics, is that in this Malavalli Block[2] alone there are 55 different kinds of co-operatives, Rs. 700,000 have been given in short term loans, and recovery is reported to be 100 per cent.[3] According to official statistics again, till March 1958, out of a total of 18,000 acres, 14,000 had been brought under the improved Japanese method of paddy cultivation. More recent figures claim it to be 16,000 acres—a truly remarkable achievement.[4]

---

[1] One palla = 180 lbs.

[2] "Block" is the unit for the organizational set-up of the Community Development programme.

[3] This is certainly not representative of the condition of the co-operative movement in the whole State.

[4] It should be clear, however, that what passes here, and often elsewhere, for the "Japanese" method is not always fully that. The genuine Japanese method involves a combination of many improvements in the details of paddy cultivation, and it is rare to find all of them being practised in the prescribed manner by the mass of peasantry in any region anywhere in India. Only one or two features of it are usually adopted. Thus in Tanjore, they told me frankly, that their method of "Japanese" cultivation begins and practically ends with transplantation of seedlings in lines (they have been used to transplanting even under their traditional method) coupled

Moreover, 87 per cent of the families own their own land in this Block so that "there is practically no unemployment, except of the educated", and that because, as Channabasappa of the village of Ragibonnanahalli put it, "once they read they do not enter the fields. They want jobs in government service. Till they can find a job, they put on fine clothes and waste their time by riding about on the bicycle and drinking coffee. Even if we offer to give them coffee at home they prefer to go out. We old people do the work and feed the younger generation these days. Education is good. But once they get it they want to go away to the town." Even so, he agrees, "since 1941 we are eating better and we dress better, though we still do not have ready cash."

Peasants in Ravani, however, claim that "there has been no improvement in our lives in the past ten years", while Bore Gowda of Banasamudram insists that "in the last ten years the poor have become poorer and rich richer". But Thane Gowda of the village of Kurikuppal is an individual example of progress. He has been cultivating sugar cane since 1933 and has eight acres of wet and two acres of dry land. In this period, he says, he has built himself a new house costing 3,000 rupees and has purchased, besides, ten *tolas* of gold and jewellery and a wireless set. He is the village "leader" and purchases 500 rupees' worth of fertilizers every year.

Similarly, residents of Hitenhally are categorical that in recent years there has been a distinct improvement in their standard of living. Their lands have been irrigated since 1942. "Before irrigation came we were getting a yield of one *palla* of paddy per acre." When the canal came it improved to eight to sixteen *pallas*. Now they are getting 18, and this year they expect to produce on an average at least 20 *pallas* per acre. This village sells a surplus of 4,000 to 5,000 *pallas* of rice per annum. Everyone, except for two recent immigrants, apparently, has land and everyone is a member of a co-operative society.

"We are able to eat well and live well", they say with folded hands. They address officials as *swamy*, which means lord. Most important of all, "we did not have coffee before. Now we are drinking coffee", and thereby hangs a tale.

---

with the use of some fertilizer and perhaps an improved variety of seed. Here in Mandya, no transplanting in lines is done, though they claim to practise everything else. Actually, the soil is so rich here that even if some fertilizer is used and the fields are irrigated, as they are, an average yield of 18 to 20 *pallas* an acre is feasible. If the complete Japanese method were employed, production could be much higher.

Hot Meals and Coffee

"Yes, that is true. Everyone has taken to drinking coffee", the women confirm. "The result is that we are unable to save anything."

Hannama, a tall, slim and intelligent woman, firmly denies that they have made any economic progress. On the contrary, she says, seemingly truthfully, "we are still struggling to clear our debts. The cost of living is high while our men go to 'hotels' and spend extravagantly on coffee and meals." She wears silver bangles, which she says were given to her by her parents. Her faded orange sari has many patches in it.

"But do you not also drink coffee and don't you have a say in the spending of money? Don't the husbands give their earnings to you to keep?" I ask somewhat timidly, afraid of intruding on a purely domestic issue on the one hand and of starting a feminist riot on the other.

"I drink coffee?" A titter runs through the women's ranks. "I have never even tasted it. No, they don't give us the money. If they do sometimes it is only to keep it, on the strict understanding that we do not touch it. They never tell us what they earn and what they spend. They enjoy themselves while we work in the fields."

And, as it turned out, it was not an isolated personal problem of Hannama alone. In these prosperous and rich districts of southern Mysore it has become general, a new social pattern of work and consumption. Previously, as among all rural communities in which both men and women work in the fields, men always left the house earlier while the women stayed back to cook. The wife then carried the meal to the farm and stayed on to work with the husband for the rest of the day. Early in the morning, before leaving, the man generally ate cold rice or *ragi* porridge kept over from the previous night. He got a hot meal only for supper. But then he was poor. Now he has more money. So not only does he himself work less—he employs more labour—but he wants good hot meals with the additional luxury of coffee in between. Coffee has become the fashion. Women, however, have no share in it. Nor has their share of the burden of work in the field or in the house been lightened. The men frankly admit to the charge. They go to hotels, not only for coffee but also for meals.

"Our women work in the fields", they say. "Then who is to give us a hot meal on time? Naturally we have to go to a hotel"—a new problem of leisured men with working wives. Their villages are built on the usual "huddling" principle of rural communities living in squalid congestion. But even a small village will boast of four, five, or even more of what are called "hotels". In reality they are simply the residence of the more enterprising villagers of the right caste, where coffee and meals are served.

"As It Has Always Been"

Moreover, with the exception perhaps of a few individuals, the consumption of surplus income seems to begin and end with less personal work in the field and with the taking of coffee and better food in a hotel and going regularly to the cinema. According to a local estimate, nearly 80 per cent of these peasants in Mandya would still be in debt. Nor is the increase in their prosperity reflected in any other visible improvement in the manner and condition of their life. Everything else is as it always was, simply "because it has always been so".

Their houses have a small, square inner courtyard surrounded by a verandah, in at least three-quarters of which cattle are tied. In the remaining one-quarter of the verandah is the kitchen, and usually the latest arrival in a cloth cradle suspended from the roof, next to the cattle. The courtyard and the verandah are naturally filthy with urine and cowdung, and straw lies all around. Outside, in a small front verandah firewood is usually piled. The rooms, one or two, are dark and open into the courtyard. Even such peasants as have been persuaded in recent years to build a separate shed for cattle will still have half a dozen of their favourite animals inside the house, so that, according to them, they can look after them all the time and feed them at night. "We have always done it." There is the superstition also that it is auspicious to see a cow first thing in the morning upon awakening. Despite all this love and reverence, however, the animals are of poor breed and emaciated.

Village lanes are generally full of stagnant pools and littered with straw, cowdung, goats, sheep and bullock carts. Drains, where they do exist, made under schemes sponsored and subsidized by the Community Development administration, are green with scum and choked with dirt. Piles of rubbish, and even big boulders at times, lie undisturbed in the middle of some of the roads.

Women wear drab checked saris. They are local handloom products; most of them have patches or big holes. The children are in rags, unwashed, their hair uncombed and matted. Men's chins are unshaven and their clothes dirty. The village of Hitenhally in this area, apart from its economic opulence recounted earlier, has had the privilege of one year of "intensive development" under a special scheme of the Planning Commission in which a full-time extension staff[1] has been assigned to it exclusively, to devote special attention to the development of "man" (and woman) as well as to his environment. Yet even this village and its people look exactly the same as others in every respect, including personal appearance, to such an extent that I am provoked to ask of them the highly impolite question as to how often they bathe. The reply is: "Once in eight days. We are all working men. What is the point of bathing?"

And although education is reportedly becoming highly popular in the district as a whole, even in Hitenhally only 90 out of its 165 children of school-going age are in school at present. The usual early morning sight on the roads here is not of children going to school, as in Kerala, but of barefooted children of six, eight, ten, collecting dry twigs for firewood and carrying small bundles of them on their heads or dragging them behind tied to a string.

[1] This is in addition to the normal extension staff of the Community Development Block, which is spread over several villages.

ANDHRA

CHAPTER VI

LAND TO THE TILLER

"FATHER was sitting right here, in this very chair, listening to the rural programme on the wireless. It was around six o'clock in the evening. Suddenly several men, accompanied by a servant of the house, rushed in from behind. As father turned to see who they were they dragged him out of the chair and hacked him into bits with an ordinary axe", Krishnayya recalls with a shudder. Yes, they hacked him into pieces, exactly as if he were a log of wood. The floor and the walls of the verandah were spattered with blood. No one thought of switching off the radio.

"We were all at home", but could do nothing, except to inform the police and to gather the limbs and pieces of flesh and consign them to the flames.

This was in 1949, in a village in Mulug *taluk* of Warangal district in Telengana, which was then in the State of Hyderabad but is now in Andhra Pradesh.[1] Narsaiyya, who was killed, was the only rich man in the hamlet. All its lands, more than 1,900 acres, were owned by him personally.

In Venkatapura, in the same neighbourhood, seven other landlords were murdered in one night. Reminiscent of the times also, in Ghanpur, in the same sub-division, is a solitary palatial manor of brick and tile where the landlord used to reside. It stands in the centre of the village, towering above the many small huts of mud and straw. The huts are peopled but the mansion lies desolate and silent. Its former occupants have migrated to the city of Hyderabad, and the big iron gates are barred in mute testimony to an era which has passed away only recently, but perhaps forever.

[1] Andhra came into existence as a State on 1st October 1953, when it was carved out of the Telegu speaking districts of Madras. Three years later it was enlarged to include the Telengana districts of Hyderabad. The old State of Hyderabad consisted of three distinct areas, Telengana, Marathawada and Karnataka. Of these

Tenants as Equals

The murders of Narsaiyya and other landowners were the outcome of a brief terrorist movement led by the Communist Party of
India.[1] Mulug was one of the worst affected *taluks* in Telengana,
which in turn was practically the worst affected area in the whole
country. Peasants killed their feudal landlords and distributed their
land among themselves in the orthodox revolutionary tradition.
Krishnayya, however, continued to live in the village, but wiser as a
result of the tragic experience, he and his brothers hastened voluntarily to acknowledge the rights of their tenants to 80 per cent of their
land, thus providing security to nearly 500 families. Not only were
the latter assured of permanent tenancy, but they were also given the
option to purchase the land they cultivated by paying for it in easy
instalments. Many of them are doing this, with the result that, as
Krishnayya put it, "Some of my former tenants have become my
equals now".

This, in fact, was the objective of the subsequently enacted
"Hyderabad Tenancy and Agricultural Lands Act" (1950). Earlier,
in 1949, all *Jagirs* had been abolished.[2] That, however, did not affect
tenant-landlord relationships nor the distribution of land. For although these *Jagirdars* had the concession to administer and collect
revenue they had no proprietary rights over the land; they were only
intermediaries between the landowners and the State. Owners were
people like Narsaiyya, who cultivated the land themselves through
employed labour, or leased it out to tenants-at-will.

The 1950 tenancy legislation sought to give security and per-
manency of tenure to the lessee, to regulate the rent paid by him, to

---

[1] At a Congress held in Calcutta in 1948 the Indian Communists adopted the
"left" strategy or what was known as the "Zhdanov line," which led to a trail of
industrial sabotage and terrorist excesses in many parts of the country. The policy
was "revised' 'in 1950 and a shift made to more peaceful methods, though violence
persisted in Telengana till 1951.

[2] By the "Hyderabad (Abolition of Jagirs) Regulation." *Jagirdars* were feudal
"tax farmers" who had the right, in perpetuity, to collect rents from large tracts of
villages. The *Jagir* was a free grant of these villages from the ruler of the State
generally as a reward for some conspicuous service.

Marathawada went to Bombay State and Karnataka to Mysore while Hyderabad
ceased to exist altogether in 1956, when all the States of the Indian Union were
reorganized on a linguistic basis. Hyderabad city became the capital of the new
State of Andhra.

impose a ceiling[1] on individual holdings, present and future, and to fix a floor—an "economic holding"—below which it should not be permitted to fragment further. It also gave the tenant an option to purchase the land he cultivated at a reasonable price fixed by the State. And then, since it was found that in actual practice only a negligible proportion of protected tenants availed themselves of the right to purchase the land, further legislation was undertaken in 1954, providing for the compulsory and automatic transfer of ownership of the land to the tenants.

In the Telengana area, however, this last provision was implemented only in Khammam district and Mulug *taluk* of Warangal district, these being precisely the regions where the peasants had been so roused politically to the full consciousness of their rights that they resorted even to murder to obtain them. As a result, about 13,000 tenants became owners of approximately 100,000 acres of land. Also, it was only in the Mulug *taluk* and Khammam district that an attempt was made to implement the provision pertaining to ceiling on existing holdings. But whereas originally a surplus of 122,000 acres of land was anticipated, subsequent enquiries indicated that it may be no more than 3,000 acres.

In the rest of the State, however, a considerable number of tenants were evicted on one pretext or another, so that even the clauses concerning the more elementary rights of tenancy were never wholly effective.[2] As a revenue official in Mehboobnagar district recalled: "Soon after the Act was passed, I was doing practically nothing except taking down statements by peasants who did not want to be registered as 'protected' tenants. They were surrendering their rights in the land they had been cultivating—'voluntarily'—even though they were entitled to protection".

Similarly, when a notification requiring landowners to declare their holdings was issued in 1954, in Raichur district, which is adjacent to

---

[1] Computed at four and a half "family holdings"—one "family holding" being equivalent to an area of land estimated to yield a gross annual income of Rs.1600.

[2] Following this Act of 1950, according to a survey undertaken by A. M. Khusro, 600,000 tenants were declared "protected" in the State of Hyderabad as a whole and they were cultivating more than one-quarter of the total cultivated area. By 1955, however, only 45 per cent of these remained as tenants; while 2·58 per cent had been evicted legally, 22·14 per cent had been thrown out illegally and 17·83 per cent had surrendered their rights "voluntarily". Only 12 per cent had purchased their lands and become owner-cultivators, thus fulfilling the intention of the law. (*Economic and Social Effects of Jagirdari Abolition and Land Reforms in Hyderabad* Dept. of Publications and University Press, Osmania University, Hyderabad, 1958).

Mehboobnagar and was at that time in the State of Hyderabad, within a year—by 1955-56—only 549 landowners out of 213,953 were found to be in possession of more than the ceiling amount of four and a half times the family holding.[1] Furthermore, whereas not a single application was filed before the Tribunal by a tenant in the whole district of Raichur for the fixing of a "reasonable rent" as provided for in the Tenancy Act of 1950, out of a total of 39,811 "protected" tenants in the district, registered immediately after the enactment of the Act, as many as 23,047 had been evicted illegally by 1955-56, while 1,688 had surrendered their tenancy rights "voluntarily". It seems no check against illegal evictions was possible as there was no response from the tenants. Had the tenants approached the local revenue official, they could have been restored their rights. Only 233 tenants in Raichur purchased the land being cultivated by them, amounting to a mere 2,976 acres.[2]

As constituted today, the State of Andhra consists of three distinct units known as Telengana, Rayalaseema and the eastern coastal districts called the Circars. Of these, although Telengana is considered to be the most backward and the southern districts of Rayalaseema only slightly less so, the Circars are the rice granary of Andhra and their peasantry its pride. In many respects the Circars are similar to Tanjore. Here are three deltaic regions of the rivers Krishna, Godavari and Pennar. The soil is fertile and extensively irrigated. Densely populated, the rural areas have a large and prosperous landed middle class, noticeably absent in Telengana and Rayalaseema.

Unlike Telengana, however, Rayalaseema and the Circars did not have the benefit of the earlier Hyderabad land reforms, since they were a part of Madras State till 1953. Whereas tenancy reform was applied to them only in September, 1956, at the time of my visit,[3] there was no law in this region to impose any ceiling on agricultural

---

[1] It is possible that this number would have dwindled further in subsequent years, according to an official note on the "Implementation of the Tenancy Act, 1950, in Raichur District". The other statistics and information pertaining to Raichur in this section are also drawn from this note.

[2] Bombay State enacted a similar enabling law (the "Bombay Tenancy and Agricultural Lands Act", 1948) which gave the tenant the right to purchase the land he cultivated. The number of tenants who exercised that right, however, in the course of the next seven years (1948-55) was only 64,609, or roughly two per cent of the total, whereas 101,053 tenants surrendered "voluntarily" their tenancy rights to 831,720 acres of land. The Act was therefore amended later in 1955, whereby tenants were automatically deemed to have become occupants of the land they were cultivating as from 1st of April, 1957.

[3] In October, 1958.

holdings. But a Bill for the purpose[1] had been published in July, 1958, and introduced in the State Legislative Assembly. The Bill proposed a ceiling holding of land yielding a net income of Rs.5,400 per annum for existing holdings and of Rs.3,600 on future acquisitions.[2]

"I have obtained the unanimous approval for the ceiling Bill from my party members in the Assembly", the Chief Minister of Andhra told me proudly—a remarkable achievement indeed, since most of the rural representatives to the legislature belong to the landowning classes, and they themselves would be adversely affected by the imposition of a ceiling on their incomes and property, as proposed in the above measure.

[1] Called the "Andhra Pradesh Ceiling on Agricultural Holdings Bill, 1958".

[2] The Bill was finally adopted only in 1960 in a modified form.

CHAPTER VII

FACTS OF LIFE

HE is tall and dark with intelligent earnest eyes, unshaven chin, no shirt—only a short *dhoti*. Most dramatically he throws down seven annas on the floor as a man throws dice.

"This is what I have earned today." He speaks in a tense voice pointing a trembling finger at the seven annas as if they had committed a crime. "My wife turned me out of the house this morning because there was nothing to eat. The only work I could find was to fish out the vessels that had fallen into the village well. The whole day I have been doing it, for which I have received this magnificent reward. We have no work and no food and you ask me about land reforms. For the last four months I have been living on only one meal a day of *bajra*. I am leading the life of a widow, helpless, reduced to pulling out vessels that have fallen into the well. What is the use? I am not bothered about your land reforms", says Hanumanthu, gritting his teeth.

He has one acre of land, on which he cultivates *bajra*. His family once owned 25 acres but lost it to the money-lender because his father had taken a loan which he was unable to pay back. That was 25 years ago. His village is in Guntur, which is one of the richest and most advanced districts in the state. In the village itself there are many wealthy landowners. Hanumanthu has a wife and five children below the age of 13. His wife also works when she is not giving birth to babies.

"We have been crying for this land reform since 1921", he says, returning to the subject once again, a little calmer. "I gave food and shelter to Congress volunteers in British times and was beaten by the police for doing so. But where is the assurance that the reforms will come even now? In the Assembly they just talk and talk. Nothing ever gets done. I know your Ministers. ——'s brother-in-law has

2,000 acres of land. Can you expect him to implement land reforms?"

"But perhaps you do not know", I venture to break in eagerly. "At a recent party meeting, the Congress[1] members of the State legislature voted unanimously in favour of the ceiling bill."

Hanumanthu glares at me with obvious contempt, as if I were unutterably ignorant, innocent even of the facts of life, and proceeds in silence to pick up one by one the seven annas lying scattered before him.

Subbarao, a local school teacher, steps in to explain in a quieter tone: "You see, practically everyone has distributed any surplus land that he had already, though the ceiling legislation is yet to come. Today, almost nobody here will be found to possess, in his own name, more land than the proposed ceiling which is expected to be imposed. Moreover, practically no tenants are left since the tenancy law[2] was passed two years ago. What is the government going to do about it?"

Tenants Become Coolies

Venkataramakrishna Rao, president of the Mandal[3] Congress Committee and himself a landlord, informs me that "due to the tenancy law the landless have been inconvenienced much more than the landlords because now the landless peasants cannot get any land on lease." In his village some 200 families have been deprived of their tenancy rights. They had been cultivating 500 acres on lease. "They are now reduced to working as casual coolies." They were, it seems, paid off and evicted. Nor will there be, according to Rao, any land to distribute here when the ceiling regulation is imposed—"At least no MLA[4] will be affected. They have all divided up their holdings already." Another man of the same village, Ram Mohan Rao, confirms: "Not a single man in this village has or will benefit by the land reforms. The tenants were so convinced that even if they went to court or to the tribunal the case would be decided in favour of the landowner that they thought it wiser to negotiate and come to terms with the landowner. So they got as much cash as they could out of him and surrendered their tenancy."

[1] The Indian National Congress—the political party-in-office in the State and in the Federal government.

[2] "The Andhra Tenancy Act", 1956.

[3] Mandal is the smallest unit in the Congress Party organization.

[4] MLA means "member legislative assembly". Every State in India has its own elected Legislative Assembly.

5. Gangadevi, member of the panchayat of the village of Hussainpur, Bihar. (Chapter XII.)

6. Villagers cleaning a drain in Arai-Keshopur, Bihar. (Chapter XII.)

7. Two Sikh refugee workmen in the cycle rim factory in Batala, in the Punjab. (Chapters XIII & XIV.)

8. A view of one of the new brick houses in the village of Edna Kalaska in the Punjab. (Chapter XIII.)

Pulla Reddy is the president of the *panchayat* in another village where two years ago there were some 800 tenants cultivating approximately 1,500 acres. Today there is not a single tenant left, according to Reddy. They have all become landless labourers. Nor will there be a single acre of surplus land to distribute in his village, he says, if and when the ceiling comes.

In Kuttumba Rao's village there are still some tenants, but they have only oral agreements—no records are kept. About 28 people here had more than the stipulated maximum of land. Now, no one has any in excess.

"There will not be an acre of land to distribute; as soon as the proposals were announced all surplus was distributed", according to Venkateshwaram, himself a landlord in another hamlet. And whereas two years ago there were at least 100 tenants in his village cultivating some 300 acres on lease, "today nobody is giving an inch of land on lease even by word of mouth."

In Bomuluru they are mostly *Harijans*. "Five years ago we were all tenants. Now we are all coolies." Says Nagindradu: "I was not paid a *pice* in compensation. I was cultivating seven acres on lease'.'

In Kapaleswaram Block, Satyanaraynan, president of another village *panchayat* board, in a pink *dhoti* and a silk shirt admits: "Previously there were at least 100 tenants in this village. Now not one." Nor will there be a single acre to distribute to the landless when the ceiling comes. The assembled landlords are calm and totally indifferent because they will not be affected by the reforms in any manner.

And so it went, in village after village, such as Atkur, Telaprolu, Veeravalli, Arugolanu, Bomuluru, Mandapeta, Jonnada, Tapeswaram, Someswaram, to name only a few. There were allegedly no protected tenants remaining in them, and there would not be any surplus land to distribute under the proposed ceiling measure, according to the residents of the villages themselves. The landowners admitted very frankly that they had taken the precaution to divide their holdings among the members of their family so that when the ceiling is imposed they will not lose any land. Only in backward and interior tracts, as in Srikakulam for example, where lands are vast and the area is thinly populated and unfertile, there may be some tenants and surplus lands still remaining, they said. But not in the rich and fertile regions of Guntur, Krishna, West and East

E

Godavari Districts, where all the above mentioned villages are situated.

As for the landless and the very small owners of minute fragments for whose benefit primarily land reforms have been designed, what is their attitude?

An Immoral Principle

"But then", asks Kallatatiah with puckered eyebrows, "how can we get other people's lands? If we are destined to be landless we must remain so." Elderly, turbaned, dark, with a white mousey moustache, Kallatatiah himself has no land. Still, he says, "I don't want any land reforms". He is cultivating two acres on oral lease now. That does not suffice, and he has to supplement his income by working as a casual labourer on other people's farms.

Velluri Satyam owns two acres and says categorically that "land reforms are not necessary".

Ramulu is young and landless. When he has work, he earns a rupee and a quarter a day. But he gets work only for six months in the year. He has heard of the reforms and is hoping to get some land. But "I want only one acre. I have five children and a wife and my mother." To my protests, he explains further that "if I am given the choice I will ask only for as much as will give me enough to feed my family". Ramulu is an ex-member of the *panchayat*. A *Harijan*, he can sign his name, but his interest in land reforms is limited by the meagre extent of his aspirations.

Iswara Reddy is also a landless labourer, young, in a vest and a very short *dhoti*. He too wants only one acre. "It will suffice to feed my family." With difficulty I persuade him that another half acre would be desirable. His anxiety for reforms is correspondingly mild.

Korra Veeranna is impressive, elderly. He owns three acres and cultivates six on oral tenancy. He positively does *not* want the reforms. "If they come, even the little some of us are still able to get on oral tenancy will be taken away", he says.

Reddy owns one acre. He welcomes the reforms in principle, but "I myself do not want any more land"—although at present he has to supplement his income by doing coolie labour.

Raju has one acre and 40 cents. He does not want any more and therefore is not interested in the reforms.

Ganga Reddy has three acres. He is more than satisfied and is totally indifferent to the ceiling proposal.

Narayana cultivates eight acres of temple lands as an oral tenant. He is not interested in, nor does he want, reforms. "If, however, others are given land I will also take some. I want only one acre. It will be enough for me."

Venkanna used to be a tenant on ten acres. An elderly man, this year he could not get a single acre on lease. He complains that no tenants are left. "We are unable to get any land even on oral contract." Now he is struggling to live by his coolie labour and on loans. On the question of land reform, however, he says: "They say some word has come that the tiller of the soil will become its owner. But I don't like such a law because it enables distribution of other people's property. I don't like it on principle. I feel it would be morally wrong."

Mahalaxmi is landless; he has a wife, mother and five children. At present, for at least four months in the year, he has no work and lives on loans which he tries to pay back from his extra earnings at harvest time. "In lean months we have only one meal a day and on several days we fast—yes, the children also." He says it casually as if it were a normal routine. His interest in reform, however, is to the extent of wanting precisely one acre of land. "The girls will go away after marriage, so it will suffice. I will not be able to cultivate more", he explains.

They all come from different villages in the deltaic districts of the Circars, precisely the region where land reforms are the most urgently needed because of the heavy concentration of landless and tenant cultivators. In Telengana and Rayalaseema areas the density of population is much lower and so is the pressure on land.

Krishnaswamy of Someswaram, however, puts an effective and final seal on the issue. He is a young man and owns 30 cents of land. Besides, he works as a coolie to support his mother and two children; he lost his wife. Yes, he has heard of the ceiling proposal but holds that: "Even if it comes I am not in favour of the principle of someone taking someone else's land and giving it to others". When I suggest that compensation will be paid to the landlord, he concedes reluctantly: "Well, if compensation is paid I would agree to take, but only with the consent of the landlord. I myself would want only one acre. Its produce will be enough for my needs. But if the land is taken away compulsorily and given to the poor, I am not for it."

"But then", he dismisses the prospect calmly with a shrug of the shoulder and without a trace of doubt or anguish in his voice, "no such law can come into force for the simple reason that no one will give up his land."

Perhaps Hanumanthu was right; I do not understand the facts of life.

CHAPTER VIII

IRRIGATION AND FLOODS

In Kurnool, in Rayalaseema, we again meet an offshoot of the Tungabhadra Project, its Low Level Canal Scheme, locally known simply as the TBP. Here also, surprisingly, the authorities are finding it difficult to persuade the peasants to make use of the TBP waters, even though, unlike their Raichur counterparts, these *ryots* have long been familiar with irrigation. This district is already partially irrigated by the Kurnool-Cudappa Canal, known as the KCC. It was constructed in 1871 by a private British company, and it also takes off from the Tungabhadra river at Sunkesula, 18 miles from Kurnool town. Almost all the KCC water is being utilized.

Now the TBP brings more water to many peasants whose lands are already partly watered by the KCC, since the two canals run parallel to each other. Far from rushing to avail themselves of the opportunity to irrigate more of their lands which were dry so far, however, many peasants are refusing to take the additional facility.

Thus in one village 500 acres are irrigated by the KCC. TBP seeks to irrigate another 380 acres, but its waters have not been taken for a single acre so far. Ramachandra Reddy, who has 15 out of his total of 100 acres under KCC irrigation, explains: "I have enough irrigated land so I have not reclaimed any more under the TBP. I am not interested in TBP." Venkataram Reddy has four acres under KCC. He could irrigate another 30 acres with TBP. But he also refuses. He simply says: "I am satisfied".

Under KCC, the main crop is now paddy, although apparently before World War II no one grew paddy despite the availability of irrigation. *Jowar* and other millets such as *korra*, *cumbu* and *cholam* were cultivated because the price of rice was low and also the people here were not used to eating rice. Their staple diet consisted mainly of *jowar* or *korra*.

According to Yella Reddy, a peasant of another village, even the

KC canal area took fifty years to develop. "People gave up their rights on the lands and went away", he says, because they could not or did not know how to cultivate wet crops. Then others, mostly immigrants, applied for and obtained their lands. "Most of the present *ryots* are not the original owners. These lands are not their ancestral properties but were acquired in this manner."

As we have seen, however, many of the present cultivators are no more interested in having additional irrigation, although according to Yella Reddy, "even coolies are eating rice now". As in Raichur, they say they will take the canal water for "dry" crops only if the rains fail. They are not interested in increasing their yields by irrigating them even when it rains. As for paddy, which must be irrigated here, they claim to be satisfied with what they are getting from the KCC irrigated lands. They do not seem to be anxious to increase the area under rice cultivation because they say the cost of levelling of land is too high.

Yella Reddy himself is an old man, over 70 years old, dark, with a very white moustache and toothless. He is vice-president of the village *panchayat*. He owns 70 acres of land, of which only eight acres are wet at present. Now 40 more acres of his have become irrigable by the TBP. But Yella Reddy has not taken a drop of its water.

Life's Labour Lost

Irrigation, of course, can revolutionize a peasant's entire life, but only to the extent that the peasant is willing. So can a flood, completely, overnight, and for many years to come. In a matter of moments it can drown a lifetime's hope and effort, and the man himself is a hapless victim.

The coastal *taluk* of Ellamanchilli, in Vishakapatnam district of Andhra, lies between a range of hills and the sea. Within two arms of the Sarada river there are some 18,000 acres of rich and fertile paddy fields. October is usually wet here, and this year it had been abnormally so.

On 21st of the month the noon-day meals were on the fire when the flood came, and it was impossible to hold it. The breaches in the protective *bund* on the river were too wide and too many. Water flowed over the embankment as well. In a matter of moments the people and their cattle were fleeing to higher lands. Entire villages were cut off and became little islands in an ocean of swirling muddy waters which flowed through village lanes like rivers.

On the seventh day of the flood we had to walk across several knee-deep channels and cross the river itself at two places where it had changed its course. While crossing it we walked over paddy fields, the paddy plants getting entangled in our toes. Everywhere was a stench of rot, and in the few fields which had emerged from under the flood the crop was yellow, turning brown. Acres and acres of fields, however, were buried deep under banks of pure white sand. Nothing will grow on them again till all the sand is removed and fresh soil is spread.

Mamidivada, a typical village, is in complete ruin. In its *Harijan* section 40 out of the 56 houses have totally collapsed. In the rest of the village many huts have collapsed and many are severely damaged. The huts here are low and single-roomed, with round mud walls and conical roofs of palmyra palm leaves with a palm trunk pillar in the centre. Now the roofs are on the ground. Pieces of bamboo, broken pottery and a rubble of earth that were the walls is all that remains. In one cottage just one portion of the wall is still standing with a wide crack right down its middle; the wall is naked but for two small, colourful Kondapalle statuettes of Krishna and Radha nailed to it side by side.

Houses, however, can and will be rebuilt. Mud and thatch are easily replaceable. But to reclaim agricultural land from sand is very difficult, particularly for a man who has no resources. These same villages had suffered from a comparably severe flood in 1928. Many of the peasants, such as Satyanarayana and Mantri Sanyasi, had then migrated to Burma or Malaya, and from their earnings there plus loans they had gradually brought their lands back into cultivation. Many of them have not yet fully repaid those loans, and once again they face the same formidable problem. Overnight their lands have become valueless. Now they are older and have larger families to support. "Moveover, we cannot return to Burma or Malaya."

A pitiable case is that of Venkadurai. For many years he had worked as a coolie in Burma. He returned home, most of the way on foot, when Rangoon was bombed in World War II. He had been saving, however, and after his return he got married and continued to work as an agricultural labourer. Meanwhile, six children were born to him, and he decided to purchase some land of his own. To his savings he added another borrowed 1,500 rupees and finally purchased one and a half acres of paddy land.

This was to have been Venkadurai's first crop of paddy from the first piece of land he had ever possessed. In a fortnight he would have harvested the crop. It had come up well.

But now it lies buried, partly under several feet of sand—he digs under to pull out a few dead plants—and partly under a deep flowing channel of water where the river has changed its course. He cannot save a single grain of that paddy, nor can he re-sow on an inch of the land. Tears roll down his deeply lined face. Four of his sons, all below ten and stark naked, stand around him, also weeping. In his arms he holds a small baby girl. He himself wears nothing but a brief loin cloth and a nose ring.

"I do not have even a clay pot left to cook in or a rag of clothing." His voice breaks.

Only the massive debt of 1,500 rupees remains. And Venkadurai is an old man now with more than 60 years behind him.

UTTAR PRADESH

CHAPTER IX

A DECADE OF DEVELOPMENT

"Nectar fell on the dead of both bands in that spot;
Bears and monkeys were quickened; the demons were not——"[1]

"IF you are writing a book you must quote this couplet from the *Ramayana*", Ujhiarelal tells me. "This is how it is with 'development'. Even though it is designed for every one and is offered equally to all only some benefit from it."

Ujhiarelal, handsome, slim and tall, in a brown shirt, *dhoti* and a Gandhi cap, is a "progressive farmer" from the Mahewa Block, the area where the first post-independence experiment in Community Development was tried, what has since become known as the Etawah Pilot Project. Villages of Mahewa Block in Etawah district have had the good fortune, therefore, of continuous developmental activity since 1948.

Diwali[2] over, the weather has just turned. Skies are pure aquamarine; sugar cane is standing in the fields, and the sowing of wheat is being completed in the vast and fertile plains of the Gangetic valley. People in these parts, even the illiterate, are highly sophisticated, inclined to speak generally in philosophic generalities, in terms no less encompassing than the universe and the universal. Maybe the wide horizons have something to do with it, for here one can see the earth dip where it meets the sky.

We sit on a *chabutra* in the partial shade of a leafy *neem*. Every house here has a raised platform in front of it where the men will sit and gossip while the *hookah* goes the rounds. There are Mahendra Singh, Mohan Singh, Birbal Singh, Arjun Singh, Nathuram, another

---

[1] *Tulsidas Ramayana*, Lankakand, Chhand 36, Chaupai 111, English translation by The Rev. A. G. Atkins, *Hindustan Times*, New Delhi.

[2] The festival of lights. It usually falls in late October or early November.

Mohan Singh, Hira Singh, Swamidin, the president of the *panchayat*, and a dozen others. Well-built men with handsome features set off by truly imposing moustaches curled up at the ends, they are all *Rajputs*, or *Thakurs*, as they are known locally. They speak in their picturesque dialect, and the discussion drifts over a wide range of topics, eventually turning into a frank and lively debate.

It is a comparatively small village with about 60 houses and a population of 500. Its streets are dirty with plenty of litter and there are piles of rubbish heaped over what were apparently meant to be compost pits. The village does not have a school of its own, but there is one less than a mile away. There is no separate girls' school in the neighbourhood, and so only four or five girls from this village attend the school with the boys—but only while they are very young.

"How can we send our girls to the higher classes? *Purdah* is bound to go one day, we know that; but it will go very slowly. Our women here still observe strict *purdah*." This accounts for the total absence of any women in the audience.

"What do you think of *purdah*?", I ask.

"I think *purdah* is good", replies *Thakur* Mahendra Singh, "simply because it has always been there. Actually, we are afraid of public opinion", he admits. "If a woman comes out into the open, everyone will say '*phirne wali aurat hai*'[1] and she will get a bad reputation."

Marriage age for girls continues to be between 12 and 14, despite the law.[2]

"Yes, we have to incur a lot of expense on a girl's marriage. When it is over we are left with nothing but our under-vests. No one can marry a daughter from his own resources; we have to borrow from the money-lender. The *Brahman*, the *Thakur* and the *Bania*—after two marriages in his family, he is reduced to ashes", says Mohan Singh shaking his head in despair. "But what is to be done? Such is *sansar*. No, education makes no difference. On the contrary, an educated boy demands a much bigger dowry than the less educated."

"Educated boys—well, they are of no use to me in the field", says Mahendra Singh, referring to his own sons. "But when I go into a government office no one will even look at me or pay any attention to what I have to say. If I take my sons with me, however, the work

[1] Literal meaning: a woman who loafs around.

[2] "The Child Marriage Restraint Act XIX" of 1929 prohibited marriage of a girl under 15 years and of a boy under 18. In 1955, by the "Hindu Marriage Act", the minimum age was again raised to 16 years for girls and 19 years for boys.

gets done in no time. They are useful there. That is why we are educating them even though we have to incur debts to do so."

Ten boys from this village are studying "Englis", as they put it.[1] Not one of them has gone back to work on the land, and even after they have completed their studies they expect to be maintained at the same standard they become accustomed to as students. Badan Singh, for example, who failed in the tenth class this year and is doing no work at present went to his father recently with a big stick and threatened to beat him unless the latter gave him 70 rupees to make a coat.

"This is our difficulty. They must have expensive coats and shoes because now they have become *genterman*. Please help us to do something about it. In less than 70 rupees our whole family is clothed for the year. But my son won't even look at *khaddar* which we all wear. He wants a coat made of foreign material. He says he will throw *khaddar* into the pond", complains the harassed father. Even so, he gave him the 70 rupees. "I had to—what else could I do?"

Consolidation, Co-operation and Corruption

Consolidation of land holdings has been completed recently in the village but they are all very unhappy about it. "It has caused a lot of trouble. Now we are embroiled in litigation in the courts", they say.

"Yes, we did have a *panchayat* committee for consolidation. But most of its members were illiterate. No one understood anything and they simply signed or put their thumb impression wherever they were told to", according to Swamidin.

"What I have to ask", says Mahendra Singh heatedly, "is this: why has consolidation been done against our will—compulsorily? We all know, now that *chakbandi*[2] has been done, that the next step will be to take away our lands. *Russibundi* will come here. Since the elephants have been killed—the British and the zemindar—how can the ant escape?"[3]

"We hear the government will take away our lands and make hotels for us where we will be given our meals." This from another in a highly sarcastic tone.

I intervene to protest that the government's policy is not communism and setting up of collective farms, but socialism and

---

[1] It means they are in secondary or high school where English also is taught.

[2] Consolidation. A special law was enacted for the purpose in 1953.

[3] They are all small peasant landowners.

promotion of co-operation in agriculture on a purely voluntary basis. They refuse to concede that it would be any different. As for the suggestion that co-operative farming would mean more prosperity, "Let us tell you a story. Once upon a time, there was a very old man. His back was bent and his joints were swollen with rheumatism. He had three sons, young and healthy. Their names were Ramu, Krishna and Sarju. One night, the old man, who was a widower, was sleeping out alone in the open on a small string cot, while the sons were inside the house, each with his respective wife. Around midnight, a couple of hyenas attacked the old man. Unable to see in the dark and too weak to defend himself or to get up and run, the father shouted for help. All three sons heard his terror-stricken shrieks, but Ramu thought Krishna would go and Krishna thought Sarju would go and Sarju did make as if to get up but his wife said, 'Why do you worry —there are Ramu and Krishna. Let them go. Must only you do everything every time?' And so it was that each, confident in his assumption that the other must have gone to the rescue of the parent, merely turned over on his side and went back to sleep. It was only next morning when they woke that they found, to their horror, the remains of their father in a field close by. That is how it will be with co-operative farming. Everyone will leave it to the other to do the work and shirk his own responsibility. In these times even blood brothers and fathers and sons are unable to live and work jointly. But we know it is coming. We are resigned to it. We know we will lose our lands", they insist. They cut in on each other to voice their feelings, which are obviously very strong.

"Yes, we all voted Congress.[1] When Pantji[2] came here he promised two things: he would abolish *zemindari* and root out corruption."

"Surely, abolition of *zemindari*[3] has made a great deal of difference to you", I suggest, "and isn't corruption much less? Did you not have corruption before 1947 also?"

"Corruption now is at least eight times to what it used to be", says Hira Singh. "As for *zemindari*, we are not very happy that it

---

[1] In the general elections of 1957 and 1952.

[2] The late Govind Ballabh Pant, first Chief Minister of Uttar Pradesh and later Home Minister in the Union Government.

[3] *Zemindari* was abolished in UP on 1st July, 1952. With it all intermediaries between the actual cultivators and the State were abolished. It was a major reform since over 90 per cent of the holdings in the State were under the *zemindari* system, cultivators on them being mere tenants with no security of tenure or other such rights in law.

has gone. We get no consideration from the government such as the *zemindar* used to give."

"We were more happy with *zemindari*", endorses another. "Now everything goes for taxes. The government takes much more.[1] On top of that, the *vikas* people come and ask us for savings. What are we to save? Where are we to get savings?"

Swamidin here steps in. "*Zemindari*'s going has to some extent been beneficial", but even he insists that "there is more injustice now. Whoever has power today wants to make money."

There is a credit co-operative society in neighbouring Anantpur. Fifty-three members come from this village. Hira Singh is its president. He complains, however, that the supervisor never looks into the papers nor does any work. "He comes only when money is being distributed or collected. We do not know anything of the accounts or what is being done. What am I to do? He never shows up."

Another member complains that loans are given to one group mainly. "We have to make three to four trips before we can get any money."

Only two men from this village have made use of the marketing co-operative last year. "We are afraid. We have no faith in it", they say.

"We have no time to take our grain there", according to Mahendra Singh. "We prefer to sell it directly though we know we can get cash as advance from the society. The trouble is that if we give to the co-operative, it means cleaning, sifting and grading grain by grain. It is too much trouble."

There is an uproar on the subject of supply of seed. "We got no seed for wheat this year, you know—very little. We have been cheated. The department is very clever. It buys from us when the grain is cheap. Like fools we sell it. And now we have to go and buy the seed in the market at exorbitant rates."

"And we know that big and influential people got all they required —in Barthena and in Anantpur", accuses Mohan Singh. "Only the poor man never gets anything. There is also favouritism in the Society. Where we wanted two *maunds* of pea seed we got only one *maund*."

"Two years ago, when the Society was started, top officials came and begged us to utilize its services. They promised we would never

[1] This is an overstatement because agriculture is not taxed heavily in India.

have any trouble in obtaining seed, and here in this very year we are in just such a quandary. Where are we to go for it now? It is not available anywhere. How can we depend on the Society? In future we will make our own seed and store it ourselves. We will not go to the Society", promises Birbal Singh.

Planning Versus Karma

"No, we have not heard of any Five Year Plan", is the astonishing reply to my question attempting discreetly to change the direction of the discussion.

"Why, don't you read *Mandir Se*?"

Mahewa Block issues *Mandir Se*, a fortnightly newspaper especially for farmers, and the secretary of every *panchayat*, who is a government official, is expected to read it out to the illiterate peasants of each village.

"We do not even know when the paper comes, who gets it and who reads it. We never collect to hear it read. We have no time. By the evening we are too tired."

Only the *panchayat* president knows something of it because he sometimes reads the paper, since it is addressed to him and he is literate. "The only thing I know about the Plan is that our lands will be taken away from us, and we, the peasants, will be destroyed", is Swamidin's interpretation.

"But do you not discuss and draw up development schemes for your own village at least?"

"Yes, we do. But they are all paper schemes. Nothing is implemented. We have nothing to show except one lane which has been lined with bricks, and that too is only half-finished." The finished portion is already crumbling.

"What about the National Savings Scheme? Haven't you contributed to that?"

"We have contributed something to Small Savings", says Swamidin, "but that is only because we have to. These officials come and ask for it. We do not give it because we want to. If we have any savings, left to ourselves we would much rather buy a calf with them. Even if they left us at that moment and asked us to send the amount later we would not send a *pice*. It is only to oblige them that we have to give."

Thanks to the Pilot Project, however, they admit that almost all of them are using improved agricultural implements here. But, "they

give us the implements, and when we go for spare parts to the Co-
operative Union in Mahewa it charges one rupee for a bolt. In Barthena I can get three bolts of the same kind in the market for one
rupee." This from one Mohan Singh, a thin elderly man who has
served in the army. He brings his plough and shows the bolt which
he has had to replace. "First I bought one from the Society[1] but it
did not fit. When I took it back the man in charge told me that if
it did not fit there was nothing more he could do about it—I could
go to Lucknow[2] for it! So then I went to Barthena and got three
bolts there for the same rupee."

But every one is using the more modern light soil plough. "The
old plough is finished." But apparently very little land has been sown
by the dibber, another improved implement that is being recommended by the Project authorities. "It takes too much time", they
say.

Birbal Singh has eight acres of land. From the Pilot Project he has
learned the art of ploughing with the fertilizer, green manuring, and
top dressing with "*alomium*[3] or whatever you call it". Though his
pre-1948 wheat average was 15 *maunds* per acre and now it is 20
maunds, he will not admit that he is earning more today because of
the Pilot Project. He insists it is due to higher prices.

"Yes, that is perfectly true", Mahendra Singh agrees. "Now
our *bhag* is better because of higher prices. Overall production is
more or less the same. If prices fall even slightly, "*to dam nikal
jat*".[4]

"Those who work hard earn more. Those who work less earn less.
This was so before 1948 and it is true now also", says Birbal, re-
lapsing into generalities. "But increase in our yields is not due to
improved techniques but to our own fate and *karma*", he asserts
firmly, with apparent conviction.

"That is precisely it", says Hira Singh with great emphasis. "It
is all a circle—light and shade. Thus, however good a *kisan* may be,
however hard-working he may be, if he has four men in the family
and they work hard, they will make a lot of money. Then if three die

---

[1] The Society is manufacturing farm implements and is supposed to sell them at
less than the market price. It has been organized by the Project, and so also have all
the rest of the service co-operatives for marketing, credit, supply of seeds, etc.

[2] The State's capital.

[3] Meaning ammonium sulphate.

[4] Literal translation: "Life goes out."

and he is left all alone, he will be finished.[1] Even if he employs servants and he has 100 *bighas* of land, he will get nothing."

"Actually our *purkhas* told us", states Mohan Singh philosophically with an exalted and far-away look in his eyes, "that in their time only four or five families would be prosperous while the rest would starve. So it is now also. The rich are the same and so are the poor. They are still poor—just as poor."

There is, for example, *Thakur* Arjun Singh, the poorest *Rajput* in this village. He has no land and lives only by selling the milk from his two buffaloes. He has a small hut where he lives with his old mother. He has not been able to marry even though he is middle-aged already, because no man will give him his daughter—he is too poor. Boys here are married normally before they are 18—"before the beard has sprouted on their chin".

There is also Ramadayal. He is sitting humbly below the *chabutra* on which the rest of us sit. He does not speak at all. When I ask him to come up and join us, the rest murmur, "let him be there". I insist, and very reluctantly he comes, but sits at a distance from the rest. The only *bhangi* in the village, Ramadayal is its scavenger—in very dirty clothes, literally hanging in shreds, unshaven, and so unkempt as to seem himself a fit subject to be scavenged.

The village has latrines here for women because of the custom of *purdah.* Men as usual go out in the fields. To clean the latrines, they need the scavenger. However, "if he refuses to work our women will also go out in the fields. We are not unduly worried."

Every household pays him, by way of wage, one *roti* a day. Besides, on all feasts and festivals he gets a little extra, and "we even marry his children by raising a subscription". He never handles any cash, since he has no other source of income. He has no land, of course. Nor does he have a separate well of his own, and "he cannot draw water from any of the village wells", though they admit that they are aware of the law on the subject.[2] "Some one else who is drawing water at the time pours it into his vessel."

[1] In this region, in Central Uttar Pradesh especially, it is interesting to note that the entire efficiency of a farm depends on the number of working men in a family. The small cultivator depends only on his own labour. Whatever is beyond the personal capacity of the family's manpower he will lease out—unofficially now. They have no other system of farm management which would enable them personally to cultivate larger areas.

[2] Articles 15 and 17 of the Indian Constitution of 1950 abolished untouchability in any form, and later "The Untouchability Offences Act No. 22" of 1955 was enacted to make the enforcement of any disability against the scheduled castes illegal and punishable by fine and/or imprisonment throughout India.

CHAPTER X

POVERTY UNLIMITED

PERHAPS Mohan Singh's *purkhas* were right. Perhaps there is an inevitability about poverty against which the individual is generally helpless—and also, at least so far, agencies of "development" as well. Take a village in the district of Ballia, in eastern Uttar Pradesh. It has had six years of "Community Development", and the Rasra Block in which it is situated has been retired into the "post-intensive" stage.

"How much gold have you hoarded by now?—tell me truthfully", I ask of Rikhi Dev, a cheerful young man with one and a half acres of land.

"Gold, you say", he laughs. "Here I do not get even two meals a day and you ask how much gold I have."

"What do you mean, you do not get two meals a day?"

"Honestly. I do not eat more than once a day", he replies.

"How often?"

"Why, always. In winter, we take only a glass of sugar cane juice during the day and in summer we drink *shira*. It is made from molasses, which we get very cheap from the sugar mill. But *shira* causes diarrhoea and so throughout summer we drink *shira* and keep running to the field. The only meal we eat is at night."

"What do you mean by 'we'?"

"We—all of us." He gestures to indicate everyone present.

"And the children?"

"They also fast during the day. If some *sag* is occasionally left over from supper it is kept overnight, and they eat it the next day but without any *roti* or rice." Even for dinner the bread is closely rationed. Milk is scarcely available because, they say, no grazing grounds are left since the abolition of *zemindari*.

"You will find it difficult to believe us", says Hardwar Ram, an elderly dignified man with a small grey moustache. "Why not see for yourself? This village has 85 houses and now it is noon. It is the normal meal time. You are welcome to go into every house and see if you can find a single fire burning or any cooked food."

And so I did. I went inside every single cottage in the village. They are small mud huts with tiled roofs. The entrance is very low and many have no doors. Inside is a small walled-in yard, lined on one side with a little verandah, and one or at the most two rooms. In each room lives a whole family. Inside the room there is usually an earthen silo for storing grain, but no other furniture. The *chula* is in the verandah; straw lies scattered in the yard; in some a little grain is drying on the floor. But in none of the 85 homes is a *chula* alight or even with ash in it. In the corner near the *chula* are piled neatly, face downward, the cooking utensils, earthen pots and a rare piece of brass. In one cottage there is a little cooked *sag* in a pan, black in colour.

The children—mostly naked, with hair matted and faces caked with dirt—stand around chewing on sticks of sugar cane and spitting out the remnants. The women are thin—their tattered sarees barely cover the body. Being of a lower caste than *Rajputs*, they do not observe strict *purdah* and they talk freely. Holding me by the wrist, they take me into their homes saying: "Come and see the tasteful dishes we have prepared for our mid-day meal", and lifting up their utensils they shake them upside down.

When I have been in all the 85 houses Hardwar Ram once again asks: "Do you believe us now? This is how it has been ever since I can remember."

To Those Who Have

Every peasant in this hamlet in Rasra Block grows some sugar cane, no matter how small a fragment of the earth he owns. Apart from its juice, which he must drink in the winter, he converts the surplus into *jaggery*, which he sells for cash to pay taxes or to purchase his extra requirements of grain. Even so, with only one meal a day and despite the various loan facilities offered by the official agencies, every family in the village is in debt to the money-lender.[1]

---

[1] The Eastern districts of UP are known generally for their greater poverty. In Ballia I discovered that one meal a day is a common routine. In the neighbouring district of Basti, *Harijans* who work as agricultural labourers are so poor that "the practice of eating *gobraha* (grains—barley, *jowar* or paddy—collected from animal excreta, and cleaned) is common. This is not considered repugnant; it is accepted

In six years of "Community Development" one drinking water well has been made sanitary in the village, and one lane has been paved with bricks. Half a dozen *ambar charkhas* have been introduced in an attempt to set up a cottage industry to supplement their meagre incomes, but the women find them too heavy to operate. "It is equivalent to grinding ten *maunds* of wheat", they say, "and even then what we earn is not worth mentioning."

Of the 85 families, 81 have land, though less than three acres. Of the four landless families, some members go as far as Assam to seek work. Those with land are finding life more difficult with the abolition of *zemindari*. As Shiv Saran, who has to feed a family of 18 members on five *bighas*,[1] put it: "Previously at least we could get additional land to cultivate on lease; even the landless could get some. Now we cannot get an inch."[2] Very few of them could assume their *bhoomidar*[3] rights, because they could not afford to pay the price, or more often, they say, because the *zemindar* compelled them to give up their rights on the land "voluntarily".[4]

Ironically, only the ex-*zemindar*—he owns land in the village though he does not live there—seems to be happy with the abolition of his *zemindari*. His *baithak*[5] is the only structure of brick in the whole village, with empty stables where his elephants used to stay in the good old days. He still owns 200 acres of land but is happy to have been relieved of the responsibility of administration, rent collection and so on which *zemindari* involved.

"There used to be too much trouble before. Now we have peace.

---

[1] One and a half *bigha* = one acre.

[2] No landowner in UP is permitted now under the law to lease out his land unless he is disabled.

[3] *Bhoomidar* used to be the tenant of the *zemindar*. By paying ten times the rent to the government he could acquire *bhoomidar* rights on the land he was cultivating. It made him its owner.

[4] When *zemindari* was abolished, the *zemindar* was permitted to retain the land which he claimed he was cultivating directly.

[5] Means literally a place meant for sitting. Since the *zemindar* visits this village often, he has this small structure where he can stay overnight also, if necessary.

---

as something ordained by fate. Eating of carrion is also common. Almost a fifth of the population of the district is compelled to resort to these abnormal practices", according to a Survey made by the National Council of Applied Economic Research, New Delhi. *Rehabilitation and Development of Basti District*, Asia Publishing House, 1959, p. 13.

We have received our compensation and we have more than sufficient land for our own needs", he tells me.

"What will happen when a ceiling is imposed?" I ask.[1]

He is not worried. "We have sufficient people within the family
to divide up the property."

Shiv Charan, on the other hand, who is landless at present, refuses
even to consider investment in land. "I would like to own my own
land, but where is the guarantee any more? Today it is one government and it has abolished *zemindari*. Tomorrow there may be
another and that may take away all land. What would I do then?
No. I would not purchase any land now even if I could find the
money."

For the rest also, they repeat with minor variations the same experiences, views, attitudes and apprehensions as those of the
peasants in Mahewa Block.[2]

"Whether it is the government or the *vikas*", sums up Hardwar
Ram finally, "it gives only to those who already have."

He might have added God to the list as well. But no—only yesterday was *Kartika Purnima*.[3] The roads were groaning under millions
of feet hastening to reach the holy Ganges for the ritual bath. Its
banks were a solid mass of humanity, while entire villages were
empty. Every conveyance was pressed into service: bullock carts,
buses, cycles and the quaint UP *ekka*, a vehicle with only a wooden
platform less than four feet square, high up on two squeaking wheels,
drawn by a miniature scraggy horse. Yesterday each of these carried
eight to twelve passengers, perched precariously and somehow
managing miraculously to hang on. Besides, a great number of people
walked—ten, 30, even 40 miles—as did also Hardwar Ram and in
fact all the men, women and children of this particular village in
Ballia, despite their empty stomachs.

But then, such is their faith, and they never seem to question or
lose it even though God might seem to fail them every day and
perhaps many times a day.

---

[1] So far no ceiling had been imposed in UP on existing land holdings but only on
future acquisitions.

[2] This was the case in almost every village I visited in the State in the southern,
central and eastern districts particularly.

[3] Full moon in the month of *Kartika*—sometime in November.

The Carpet Weavers

Not quite all the villages were empty on the occasion of *Kartika Purnima*. At least one was not; not from lack of faith but because its inhabitants have to work every day in the year for sheer survival. Hussainipur has 32 houses; its men are engaged not in agriculture but in an industry, carpet weaving. Every loom in Hussainipur is working today even though it is *Kartika Purnima* and everyone else is going for a bath in the Ganges.

Carpet weaving has been a full-time traditional occupation with the people of Hussainipur since the time of the Moghals, who introduced the craft. The weavers are all professionals, each having learned the craft from his father. They do only the weaving in their homes. Trading is done by others, individuals and companies who also provide raw materials and designs, handle the marketing and pay the weavers piece wages, according to work done. Every year these hand-woven carpets worth several millions of rupees are exported to different countries in the world. One square yard of such a carpet may cost in the market anything from 100 to 400 rupees per square yard, depending on the quality. Yet the weavers' wage a square yard comes to only about three rupees and four annas. And it is divided among four or five men who work simultaneously on a single loom, explains Shridhar, a slight small man with one eye. "Working from morning till night, till the very last ray of daylight, and taking time off only for a quick bath and a meal, we are able to weave on an average nine inches in a day."

There is no electricity here, and their feeble oil wicks do not suffice for working at night. No minimum working hours are observed. In winter they may be eight; in summer ten, even twelve. Ten days in the month may be spent in setting the loom, for which they earn no wages. So the average income for a weaver works out to four or at the most eight annas a day. Normally a family with two men working full time at the loom earns between 15 to 30 rupees in a month. Children are put to work for two to three years as apprentices and paid nothing. They start from the age of seven, or sometimes earlier, and therefore do not go to school. Every man in the village is in debt to the company or individual he weaves for.

Any slight defect in the weave and wages are cut, they say. "Whereas the bigger companies at least pay regularly, private traders are mostly dishonest. If they fail to sell the goods, they hold back our

wages on one excuse or another or cut them drastically for no fault
in the weave. The company might pay us higher wages. But private
traders will not allow it. They are influential people—some are
politicians or related to politicians." They name them. "So, you
see, they can get everything done in their favour. No one listens to
us, even though we have a Union of all the carpet weavers and we
went on strike for a month. Nothing came of it."

Nearly 12,000 looms are employed in this industry, spread over
villages like Hussainipur in four districts of Uttar Pradesh—Mirza-
pur, Varanasi, Jaunpur and Allahabad.

The Silent Grindstone

Dukhi[1] Ram, so appropriately named by a perhaps equally suffering father, has twelve members in his family. Three men in the
family work on the loom, yet their total income is only one rupee a
day.

"We work very hard", Dukhi Ram says earnestly. "but our
stomachs are never full."

It is true. His own stomach is a hollow. In fact, the whole village
population looks frighteningly underfed. A peasant at least has the
advantage of growing, even if only partially, his own requirements of
grain; or if he is landless his wages are normally paid in kind. These
people have to purchase all their food in the market at the high prices
now prevalent.

The village, too, is in a condition of desolation; it could pass for
an archaeological ruin, except that it is still lived in. It is well off
the main road, or any road of any kind. Many houses are crumbling.
A few are of brick, "made by our forefathers"; most are of mud.
The loom takes up a whole room and goes deep into the ground and
right up to the ceiling. Sometimes the loom collapses, bringing the
roof down with it, and "one or two men are killed".

The streets are full of refuse. A few buffaloes are tied in the
narrow unpaved lanes. Two carpets, soft and of beautiful design
with red, blue and yellow flowers, have just come off the loom and
lie in the open in the shade of a mango tree, ready to be taken to the
company's godown.

"May I come in?", I ask the wife of Shridhar, master weaver.

She is young, with a sweet round face which she covers partially.
The red cotton sari which she wears, though it has many holes and

---

[1] Means sorrowful.

patches, sets off her pale skin rather well. She merely nods to invite me in. She has two children, and one of them obviously has an enlarged spleen. She does not take him to the doctor "because he demands money".

Her small single room has a *kutcha* floor, uneven and broken. There is no carpet, no furniture either—not even a cot. There is only a black earthen pot on the *chula* and in the *chula* there is some ash and a small stump of wood. In another corner opposite there is a stone *chakki*. They have no land and she does no work outside the house.

"You work on the *chakki*?"

She nods and then with eyes still downcast she murmurs in a very low whisper: "I can work on it only when there is something to grind. How can I grind when there is nothing to grind?"

"Why? Doesn't your husband bring you every day at least some grain to grind?"

She looks up fully for the first time. Her black eyes, thickly fringed with long curling eyelashes, are brimming with tears. She shakes her head, and a tear rolls down her left cheek. She turns her head away and covers her face.

BIHAR

CHAPTER XI

IN THE LAND OF THE BUDDHA

STONE grinds on stone and the anguished echo goes back in time to more than 2,500 years ago when a prince became a mendicant to seek an answer to human suffering.

It was in what is now known as the State of Bihar that Gautama searched and found the answer to his quest on a full-moon night in the month of *Baisakh*[1] and became the Buddha. Here was Rajgriha,[2] the capital of the kingdom of Magadha, ruled by Bimbisara, where Buddha spent many years both before and after his enlightenment. It was here that the first Buddhist Council met soon after the Master's death. In Bodh-Gaya is the *bodhi* tree under which Gautama spread the grass given to him by the grass-cutter, Sotthiya, on the fateful night when, facing east, he sat in deep meditation till he attained *Samma Sambodhi* or "Supreme Enlightenment". Close by flows the river Niranjana,[3] which the sage crossed to reach the *bodhi* tree, after taking food from Sujata, a poor girl, in the village of Senani. On its left bank is the Muchalinda Lake[4] where Buddha took his bath and was overtaken by a furious storm. Muchalinda Nag, the local serpent king, protected him with its hood till the storm abated.

Though he preached his first sermon in the Deer Park at Sarnath, near Benares, where he propounded the four noble truths and the eight-fold path whereby humanity could work out its deliverance from the stresses and sorrows of the world, Buddha returned to Bihar, where he spent most of the remaining 45 years of his life propagating the new *Dharma*. He preached to both high and low, the prince and

---

[1] In May.

[2] Now known as Rajgir.

[3] It is now called Lilajana.

[4] It is now known as Mucharin tank and it belongs to the village close by of the same name. It is one mile from Bodh-Gaya.

the peasant. He strove to remove caste, fear, superstition and mean-
ingless rituals, which serve only to exploit the ignorant. He taught
the beauty of love and compassion, the need for rationalism, truth,
ahimsa, and equality as habits of thought and outlook and practice in
daily life.

That was 2,500 years ago.[1] Today the landscape survives, but the
light has faded from it, and once again the struggle on the socio-
economic level appears to be against the identical forces of obscurantism which the Buddha strove to combat on the moral and religious
plane.

Thus, not very long ago, in the village of Mucharin, one Gopal
Prasad went to work on a *bund* on the river Lilajana. According to
him: "It became late and I decided to spend the night at the *bund*
and not return to the village. I am a *Koeri*[2] by caste. Some other
people also were camping there for the night but they were all
Bhoomiyar Brahmins. Since I had not taken anything with me, they
told me to cook and eat in an old earthen pot which was lying in the
sand. I was told that that pot had been used by a *Koeri* before, so I
could use it. But it looked very dirty and old, and I thought to myself,
how am I to be sure who had used it. Since the *Bhoomiyars* were
cooking their meal, I decided to eat the food cooked by them, and
did so. They gave me some. Next day there was an uproar in the
village. They called me insane and threatened to excommunicate
me; they wanted to beat me up. My family also turned against me.
Not a soul would take my side. Even if a *Harijan* was working the
latha[3] on the well I could not bathe there. All this because I had
eaten food cooked by a *Bhoomiyar*. I was young then, and it made me
angry. So I ran away to Gaya.[4] There I stayed with a tailor and
learned the trade. For more than a year I lived in exile. The *purohit*
advised me to have my *shuddhi* done, but I was obstinate. I decided
to fight it out, even if it meant that I could never return to the village.
Since I had become independent economically I did not really care.

"Then, fortunately for me, my grandmother died, and the priest
advised me to utilize the opportunity to undergo the rites of purification as well. I agreed and went to Vishnupad temple in Gaya and had

---

[1] Around three centuries later it was again from his capital at Pataliputra in Bihar
that Emperor Ashoka made Buddhism the State religion so that it spread to every
corner of India and beyond.

[2] A sub-caste of *Sudras*.

[3] Irrigation device.

[4] District headquarter town.

my head shaved. I had to do that in any case for my grandmother, and then the *purohit* did my *shuddhi* also. Only then was I accepted back in my caste and family."

What is more, according to the villagers, this rule that a low caste should not eat the food of a *Brahmin* (normally it is the other way about) is not in a spirit of retaliation or assertion of equality, but to protect the *Brahmin* and to enforce due respect for him. Because if a low caste eats his food it would not imply contamination, but in cooking for him the *Brahmin*'s hands might be burnt and this cause suffering to the *Brahmin*. A *Koeri* is not considered worthy of it. Within the multi-caste village community of Mucharin of today there is normally no inter-caste dining nor social intercourse even within the upper castes "unless there is some special occasion when *pukka khana* is served", this being permitted under the caste rules. But under no circumstances "would we eat with the *Harijans*".

Why Should I Plough?

It is pure obscurantism again which in Bihar, as in most parts of India, continues to prohibit certain upper caste Hindus from touching the plough, though these communities are full-time agriculturists and often own, except in predominantly tribal regions, most of the best cultivated land. This has serious economic repercussions.

In the village of Dhobgama, in Darbhanga district, for example, there are several *Brahmin* landowners. Although in most cases their land holdings are small, every one of them has given some land to a *Harijan*, to build his house on and to cultivate it on a crop-sharing basis, or entirely for himself.

I asked these landowners how it was that *Harijans* could get land from them to cultivate, since the present trend generally is not to give any land on lease because of the tenancy laws. At first one of them said: "Well, after all they have to live also. Where will they go if we do not give them land?" When I enquired again if it was only out of altruism that they gave the land, to keep the *Harijans* alive, another reason emerged: "But if they go away, what will we do? Who will work for us?" It is because not one of these *Brahmin* farmers ploughs, or is permitted by caste custom to plough and work on the land.

Jogeshwardas, of another village, admitted frankly: "You see we are *Maithili Brahmins*, so we cannot plough. To bind the *Harijans* to ourselves we give them the land. Then they have to work for us exclusively, and only when we have no work can they work elsewhere. Otherwise, what would we do if they went away? The land would remain unploughed."[1] If the landowner's property is sufficiently large, then the labourer's whole family is tied down to working for him. If not, then some of its members can work for others.

The land given to *Harijans* in this way—it varies between two to eight *kuttas*[2]—is in lieu of wages and to ensure their not leaving the landowner in the lurch at the crucial time of ploughing.

Though the system enables the *Harijan* labourer to obtain a minute piece of land to cultivate and to build his house upon, it also reduces him to a very unenviable position. It virtually immobilizes him,[3] so that as Nanu Chamar, a labourer of Balha said: "My wages are the same today as they were ten years ago". Should he ask for more, or for the freedom to work elsewhere, the landlord will not only deprive him of the land he has given him to cultivate but will also order that the *Harijan* take his house off his property. The house is only a wretched mud hut, but it must have a spot of earth, however small, to stand upon. And merely exchanging one landlord for another does not materially alter the basic situation.

There is on the State's statute books a law[4] to protect such agricultural labour against eviction. However, that does not prevent the landlord from threatening him, knowing that the man has neither the gumption nor the economic strength to go to court, especially if, as is invariably the case, he is also indebted to the landowner. In that event, even if the labourer should muster courage to leave or shift his homestead, he must first repay the landlord's debt before he leaves. This he can seldom hope to do, because, for one thing, his wages are never paid in cash, and, secondly, the grain which he receives in wages or which he raises on the land he is given does not

---

[1] Here, as elsewhere, *Harijans* constitute most of the agricultural labour. 86 per cent of the population of Bihar depends on agriculture, while 93·3 per cent lives in the rural areas. Agricultural labour families constitute 40 per cent of the State's rural families, inclusive of the class of "attached labourers" described above.

[2] One acre = 22 *kuttas*.

[3] Although certain sections among the Biharis emigrate regularly to other States in search of work, it is mostly "distress" emigration. "The volume of inter-district movements appears to be relatively small. Over 92 per cent of the population remains in the home districts and are immobile even in the slack agricultural seasons." (*Techno-Economic Survey of Bihar* by National Council of Applied Economic Research, Asia Publishing House, 1959, p. 16).

[4] The "Bihar Privileged Persons Homestead Tenancy Act" (1948).

suffice even to feed his family. There is never any surplus. Moreover, thanks to the abolition of *zemindari*[1] and other tenancy reforms, he is unable now to supplement his income by taking on extra land on lease. As the two *Harijans*, Dukhadas and Akhloo, said: "We could get more land on *batai* from the *malik* before—before the abolition of *zemindari*—but not now. At times we cook twice a day. But there are days we do not cook at all. Our stomachs are never full."

Even now, the landlord is virtually the only source of loans to the landless labourer. Official agencies are there, of course, but the landless peasant is unable to make use of the credit facilities offered by the government because, firstly, he has no "credit-worthy" security to offer—he has nothing to pledge except his and his children's labour, which the government will not accept. Secondly, no official agency is prepared at present to lend him money, as the landlord does, for such "unproductive" causes as births, deaths, sickness, hunger and the inevitable marriage in the family. These are precisely the regularly recurring occasions for expenditure which the hapless labourer can neither avoid nor afford to meet out of his own resources, and they constitute the main cause of his debts.

In this manner,[2] not only does the labourer become rooted for life, sometimes generations, like a tree on literally a few square feet of earth which is never his own, but farming efficiency suffers[3], because a man who does not work himself can seldom be a good farmer—and all because an obsolete prejudice, in spirit quite contrary to professions of either democracy or socialism, stays entrenched because of caste tradition and because it continues to "work". As Sitaram Thakur said, perhaps not illogically: "Why should I plough when I can get another man to plough for me?".

---

[1] Abolition of *zemindari* was completed in Bihar by 1st January, 1956. The entire State was covered by this system of permanent rent-farmers under the "Permanent Settlement Regulation" of 1793. By 1956 all intermediaries between the government and the cultivators had been removed under the "Bihar Land Legislation Act". It gave 22·5 million peasants permanent and heritable security of rights against eviction or enhancement of rent.

[2] Variations of this system exist in some of the other States as well.

[3] In Bihar State as a whole 46 persons are employed in agriculture for every 100 acres of gross area sown as against the all-India average of 31. Not only is the per capita output consequently low, but the average yields per acre in Bihar are practically the lowest in India. This, despite the fact that Bihar plains are among the most fertile agricultural tracts in the country.

CHAPTER XII

PANCHAYATS AND VILLAGE LEADERS

MANY aspects of belief and superstition in the villages of Bihar today are closely akin to those of 2,500 years ago, and one of the steps the State government has taken to inject some fresh dynamism into the rural communities has been to create elected village councils known as *panchayats*.[1] These have been entrusted with certain responsibilities, such as revenue collection, village administration, social welfare, and execution of local development works in co-operation with the State's Community Development organization and other branches of the administration.

The *panchayat* of Jethian, a picturesque village nestling deep in the forest of Rajgir valley, for example, has been entrusted with the responsibility of collecting the land revenue. It is a rich *panchayat* and is working well.

"But we are afraid", they say. Tax collection is an unpopular job anywhere in the world, and an elected body can never exert as much pressure as may be necessary. "People are generally unwilling to pay, and so far we have been able to realize only 25 per cent of the dues", says Ashok Kumar.

As for "development" work, in Balha, the residents of the village admit frankly that the roads and buildings, though made by them under the Community Development programme[2] and involving a good measure of *shramdan*, are not maintained by anybody. "We make them because we are told to, and then *takat rahat hain*[3] in the expectation that the Block Development Officer will repair them."

---

[1] The state of backwardness of course is not peculiar to Bihar. The creation of *panchayats* also is an all-India phenomenon, though the powers and functions of the *panchayat* vary between the different States.

[2] It has been in a Community Development Block since 1952.

[3] "We sit back and watch".

In this village they have constructed a building for their primary school, for example. It is a single hall, and it was made only a couple of years ago. But already the roof is sagging and it leaks, so that the teacher has to declare a holiday whenever it rains. But no one takes the initiative to repair it.

Similarly, in Mucharin, neither the *panchayat*'s record nor its attitude toward "development" is exemplary, though comparatively speaking it is a rich village and has been in a Community Development Block since 1953. "The *panchayat* is not working well", the villagers themselves tell me. "It could do a lot of useful work if we all worked together." But there are two factions within the village.

The approach road to Mucharin is in a very bad condition, but the *panchayat* members say: "Only the government can improve it." The major development work undertaken here is an underground drain which has resulted in the paving of the main streets with bricks. The government gave part of the money, while the rest was to be a contribution from the villagers, who were also in charge of its construction through the *panchayat*.

"This has been a great gain", they tell me. "Previously one could not walk in these lanes for the dirt and the slush."

But though most of the drain has been completed, 500 feet of it has lain unfinished for the last three years. The basis of people's contribution had been that each should give for the stretch in front of his own house only. Where the row of houses ends, responsibility ends— even though to reach the paved street one has to walk through stinking slush and pools of filth and water. This flows into the approach lane and from there into the tank in which the Buddha took his bath.

Problem of Leadership

To a large extent the success or failure of a *panchayat*'s work rests on local leadership. And it can make all the difference if it is "traditional"; for, although *zemindari* has been abolished most of the ex-*zemindar* families continue to wield a great deal of influence in the estates they once owned, the relationship between them and their old tenants still being largely feudal.

There is, for example, a village Dosma, whose *panchayat* has elected a woman as *mukhia*—perhaps the only village to do so in the whole State of Bihar. She is a widow. It would have been a remarkable sign of progress had she been elected because she is a woman, since in Bihar, in the villages particularly, most upper caste women

are still in *purdah* and educationally, all women are very backward.
However, she has been elected essentially because she is the widow
of the ex-*zemindar* of this area. Her large, double-storied house, of
traditional design, stands apart and towers above the rest of the cottages of thatch and mud. She herself is known as the *malkin* or
mistress. She was persuaded to accept the post of *mukhia*, mostly by
official pressure, because the local *panchayat* was riven between two
powerful factions, and there was no other way of bringing them
together. "If the other two candidates had been permitted to contest
there might have been broken heads." When she agreed to stand,
they both stepped down, and the result is that this is now one of the
smoothest working *panchayats* in the district and the State.

And yet, the *mukhia* herself never attends meetings of the *panchayat*, nor does she show herself publicly, because, as a *Rajput*
daughter and wife belonging to a rich *zemindar* family: "In this, my
house, I never used to step beyond the doorstep of my room, let
alone that of the house—unless it was absolutely necessary. I just
ate and slept; I had no other work." When she visited relations in
another village, her face would be completely covered, "first with the
sari, and over that I would have a *chaddar*. When walking, I had
to manage to see through the sari. I could not even uncover one eye."

She used to be carried in a palanquin, which again was completely
wrapped by a thick red cloth. Four *kahars*[1] bore the palanquin on
their shoulders and were accompanied by six armed sepoys as guard.

"Now when I have to go anywhere I go by *doli*,[2] but I venture out
very seldom because it is much too costly. Then we used to pay two
pice per *kahar*. Now we have to pay each man two rupees."

When her husband died in 1944 there was no adult male member
in the family to take care of the affairs of the *zemindari*. Even so, for
three years she continued as before, in total seclusion, only to find
that her estate was going to ruin. So she began to exercise control
and give direction, though still from inside the house. "Necessity
impelled me." She has never been to school but can read a little
Hindi and can sign her name.

To take care of the *panchayat* she has nominated an agent, who
presides over its meetings and also attends the Block Advisory Committee meetings on her behalf. Unlike many *mukhias*, she is not

[1] A sub-caste of *Sudras*.

[2] There are still no roads around this village, which is nearly ten miles from the
main road. Even a jeep can reach it with difficulty and only in the dry weather.

interested in making money for herself nor in taking sides in village factions and local politics. She is both rich and pious, and because she is the *malkin* she commands unquestioning respect. Thereby she is in a position to run the village council harmoniously, even though by proxy.

Another *panchayat*, in Arai-Keshopur, is doing good work, but for a different reason. This village is deep in the interior and inaccessible. But the people here have had the advantage of a different kind of leader, a political worker from Uttar Pradesh who absconded in the 1942 "Quit India" movement and came to Bihar disguised in the saffron robes of a *sadhu*. He stayed on as a *sadhu* in Arai-Keshopur, and has been doing excellent rural uplift work in this and surrounding villages independent of the official Community Development programme, from which, he says, his approach is different, in that he neither demands from the villagers the fulfilment of any targets, nor does he give them anything except advice—no subsidies or loans. He himself holds no office, though because of his saffron robes he undoubtedly enjoys a very useful moral authority. He merely creates an atmosphere, he claims, and persuades the people to "want sufficiently" to find the means and do the job on their own. According to the people themselves: "Development started in our village only in 1942, when *Swamijee* came and began to live here. We began with education. We are all educated today due to his efforts." Nearly 40 per cent of the adults have become literate, and there are six graduates now in Arai-Keshopur.

Before 1942 there was only a small elementary school in a private house with a District Board teacher. By 1950 Arai-Keshopur had established a Senior Basic School, towards which the villagers contributed 5,000 rupees and five acres of land. The villagers also made a *Samaj Bhawan*[1] with a library, and they are running a multi-purpose co-operative society, which does both welfare work and business for profit. It has constructed 700 feet of drainage in the village as well as water troughs for animals. Their *panchayat* has been popularizing horticulture and kitchen gardens, for which it received the first prize in 1957 in a district competition. The whole village, including the *Harijan* section, has an exceptionally neat and clean appearance. The *Harijans* themselves say that if I had come 15 years earlier I could not have stood near their homes for the dirt and the stench.

Baldev Singh, the *mukhia* of the *panchayat*, explains that "one

[1] Community Centre.

feature of our work is that we take no government loans. Not one man in this *panchayat* has taken *taccavi* from the government. We arrange to lend to each other within the village, interest free. Fertilizers also are sold here but not given on credit."

"We made a well for *Harijans* for 200 rupees, which would have cost the government at least 600. We could do it cheaply, because the *Harijans* made their own bricks. They had to pay only for skilled labour and the cement."

And so continues the list of improvements. They also have a community radio set, and a dispensary which they run themselves. Yet this village is not even covered by a Community Development Block.

The Story of Two Community Centres

Both these *panchayats*, of Arai-Keshopur and Dosma, are thus working efficiently and smoothly, primarily due to effective leadership. Both have concrete work to their credit—Arai-Keshopur more because it started working on these lines much earlier, in 1942.

In Dosma, however, a community centre is under construction under the auspices of the Community Development programme, for which the government has contributed half the money. The rest is to be the villagers' contribution. It is an impressive building, big and solidly made of brick, coming up rapidly at the entrance to the village. It cannot be missed. The walls are already up.

As we sit in the verandah of the *mukhia*'s house opposite, I point to it casually and ask the villagers what it is they are making. They look at each other in consternation. It seems no one knows. Then one of them says they are going to have a hall.

"Why are you making it?" I ask again.

Silence.

I ask each of them, one by one: "Have you contributed to it by giving cash or labour?"

Yes, each of them has.

"Why?"

No one knows. They are all confused by now. One of them picks up courage to say that he helped because the *malkin* had said it should be made—"but I do not know why".

Then another man says: "It is being made for the *hakims*[1] to sit in. Since they have started coming to the village[2] they need a *katcheri*

[1] Referring to government officials.
[2] That is since the work of Community Development started.

G

to hold meetings in." That seems to them the most plausible reason and it is readily endorsed by the rest.

In Arai-Keshopur also the *Harijans* have made a community centre, a separate one of their own, apart from the main *Samaj Bhawan* of the non-*Harijans*. It is a very humble building with no plinth, only mud walls and a thatch roof—just one room. There is no furniture inside, only the ashes of a burnt-out fire in one corner. Nobody gave them any assistance or subsidy to build it because, as already stated, this village is not covered by an extension Block. We were standing beside it as the *Harijans* of the village complained loudly of their poor economic condition. Their houses are clean, but their clothes are in shreds and their children are naked, although it is the cold season now. In their relationship with their landowning employers they face the same difficulty as most *Harijan* labourers elsewhere in the State. In fact, they are even more bitter about it, because only eight to ten miles away, they say, the wages are substantially higher. But they can neither go away nor improve their lot in their own village, but must continue to work for the same landlord and on his terms.

"We are starving", they were telling me in frenzied voices. "How was it ten years ago? Well, the rich have become richer and the poor poorer. That is the fact. We are not any better off."

Then I interrupted and, pointing to the community hall, I asked them who had built it.

There is an immediate drop in the temperature and a change in the tone. "Why, we!" is the reply.

"Why? Whatever for? Who told you to build it?"

"No one."

"Then why did you build it?"

"Well, many pilgrims pass by this way to go to Rajgir.[1] They can stay in it. We also can meet inside it. We sit there in the evenings whenever we want to, especially in the cold weather. For sitting outside we have made this *chabutra*."[2]

"But you were just telling me that you are always hungry and so poor. Why did you then bother to put up this structure—it must have meant so much extra work and expense?"

---

[1] Rajgir is famous for its hot springs, to which many people go in the hope of cure for certain types of diseases. Also, besides being a centre for Buddhists, Rajgir has places of pilgrimage for Jains, Muslims and Hindus as well. Arai-Keshopur is about 13 miles from Rajgir.

[2] A platform round a tree.

"Oh, it meant only work which we did in our spare time. No expense really," a woman with black curly hair replied, with a look of such pride that the hall might well have had marble walls.

Public Opinion

Apart from the quality of leadership, which necessarily varies with individuals, the enduring factor which is required to ensure the healthy functioning of a *panchayat* is an effective public opinion[1], the underlying operative principle of all democratic institutions. In a village, where the community is small, one assumes it is able to exercise sufficient control and supervision.

And yet in Mucharin, when it emerged that none of the village works had been executed honestly by the *panchayat*, the members of the electorate could only say: "Well, we know he and he and he cheated. But what should we do? Knock them on the head? Kill them?" Vasudeva Mahto simply put the blame on human nature. "Now the times are such; what is to be done? People have become more selfish. The educated are worse. We do not know why. *Prakriti* is changing perhaps. It is beyond our ken—supernatural. God alone knows."

How keen and effective is this crucial element of public opinion I had occasion to witness at Bishenpur, where a newly elected *panchayat*—executive and judicial—was being sworn in to succeed what had previously been only an *ad hoc* council.

A *shamiana* has been erected. At one end of it stands a wooden divan and a table with the usual unpolished brass vase with withered flowers. A district official performs the ceremony of inauguration and oath-taking by the light of a petromax lamp, which needs constant pumping. He also gives an eloquent speech on the duties and responsibilities of the members of a *panchayat* and of the village community.

Yet the audience seated on the floor consists of barely 15 people and no women are present, although on the executive of the *panchayat* there is a nominated[2] woman, a most charming person of about sixty, Gangadevi by name. The *panchayat* covers a population of about 4,000 people, but only 15 of them are present to witness its

---

[1] Apart from official supervision which also is not always reliable or efficient.

[2] In Bihar only the *mukhia* is elected by the general body of villagers. The *mukhia* then nominates his executive and is expected to include at least one woman. Members of the judicial council however are all elected. A government official, a trained Village Level Worker, acts as the secretary to the *panchayat* executive.

inauguration. Not only is there practically no audience, but eight of the members of the *panchayat*—the *panchs* themselves—are also absent.

As for the main problem of this *panchayat* and the villagers' attitude towards it: "Every village here has an *ahar*. But it has no water in it because ever since *zemindari* was abolished no one has maintained these tanks and so they have silted up.[1] The result is that if there are no winter showers now our *rabi* crops wither away", explains the *mukhia*. Young, nondescript, educated up to the secondary school, he has only two acres of land, but is the solitary exception to be dressed in white clothes of fine quality in an assembly of dirty and coarse apparel. He represents the typical mediocre "professional" village leader who claims he does "nothing except *panchayat* work to serve the people", but enjoys neither the traditional prestige of an ex-*zemindar*, nor the moral status of a *sadhu*.

"Who maintained these *ahars* previously?" I ask.

"The *zemindar*'s agent used to get it done. The *zemindar* saw to it that everyone got the irrigation water and so we used to be certain of reaping good harvests. Now it is the government's responsibility, but the government simply passes orders. Nothing gets done", is the reply.

"In Bashaita there are four wells from the time of the *zemindar*", says the representative of that village. "In his time they were being repaired regularly. Now they are all filled up and we have no water. We are suffering terribly."

"What is your plan?" I ask the *mukhia*.

"Please give us a canal", he pleads with folded hands. "For the past three years our crops have been failing regularly." He has no other plan.

"But why do you not repair the wells and *ahars* yourself if the government does not do it, instead of waiting for a canal and letting your crops wither in the meantime? Didn't the *zemindar* repair them with your labour, by compelling you to contribute *begar*? Can't you do the same now of your own free will?"

They—the *mukhia*, members of the *panchayat* and the rest—do not think so. "What are we paying the government taxes for?" they say. "Why should the government not do it?" is the attitude of all. As for

---

[1] According to the local officials, it is the general problem in this whole district of Gaya, which is covered by an excellent system of minor irrigaton works maintained previously by the *zemindar*.

begar or free labour, which they gave to the *zemindar*—"Oh we did not mind it. We used to be given *chana* and *gud* for lunch, and at least the 'works' were maintained. Now it is the government's responsibility. Why should we do it?"

In despair I turn to petite, toothless Gangadevi. She wears a thick cotton sari with a red border. Though illiterate, and a *kaharin* by caste, she is full of wit and practical wisdom and can quote chapter and verse from the *Ramayana*.

"Well, what do you think are the prospects of this *panchayat* working well and efficiently?" I ask of her.

She thinks for a while and then says gravely: "The fact is that people here are not inclined to co-operate or work together for a common cause—for any community work. How then can a *panchayat* work in the absence of such a spirit?"

"What about you? You seem so wise?"

"I believe that whatever one has, one must share with those who do not have. After all, I can't take it away with me. He who gives will give more if He wants to."

Though she has only five *bighas* of land, part of which is mortgaged, and only one bullock to plough the land with, yet, "if I find a man stealing maize from my fields I take back just one or two stalks from him to impress upon him that it is mine and that it is wrong to steal, but I allow him to take the rest", because she feels that he must need it very badly if he is driven to steal it.

"But that is not the case here with these people," she says jerking her head towards them. "One can die from want but no one will lift a finger to help." She holds up the small finger of her right hand. "Besides", she says lowering her voice to a confidential whisper and placing her hand lightly on my elbow: "Do you think any one of them is capable even of thinking or talking any sense?"

"Yes, of course I will talk. But then", she adds without the slightest trace of conceit or arrogance, though with an unmistakable sparkle in her bright eyes, "what can one person do? Can one *bania* make a bazar?"

She looks into my eyes for a moment in silence, and then smiling her charming toothless smile repeats softly: "Tell me, can one *bania* ever make a bazar?"

PUNJAB

CHAPTER XIII

MOBILITY OF THE UPROOTED

"WE came in the clothes we were wearing. Our only luggage consisted of cooked food for ourselves and rations for the animals. Of all our animals we brought with us just the two bullocks yoked to the cart. We come from the districts of Multan, Montgomery and Lyallpur. We did the whole 200-mile journey in our bullock carts.

"When we arrived here, in October 1947, this village was in ruins. It was a Muslim village and it had been burnt and looted. Not a single house was intact. Only two of them were of brick, and of those only the naked walls were standing. Land had been cultivated but the crop had been cut. We found a little maize standing, which we harvested. There were 25 percolation wells, but 20 of them had no water.

"The first thing we did, once the lands had been allotted to us,[1] was to install tube-wells. We were not used to irrigating from wells, because in Pakistan we had canals. We did not relish the idea of walking round and round with the Persian wheel. One of our men actually fell into the well while doing so. But then there was no electricity here. So we formed a committee, collected 20 rupees per head, and applied for power. Niranjan Singh and Badan Singh were assigned to do the running around in the various offices, and, finally, we obtained the necessary sanction. For tube-wells the government offered loans, not subsidies.

"We were so impatient that we did not allow the electricity department to install the line. As soon as the materials started arriving at the railway station we told the officials that there was no need for their hired labour doing 'hay ho, hay ho'. We would do the job

---

[1] Refugees from Pakistan were allotted agricultural land in proportion to their respective holdings in Pakistan.

ourselves. You see, we wanted to see the tube-wells working over-night, and you know how slowly the administration works.

"So we fetched the materials in our own bullock carts. Over a stretch of three miles we dug the pits for the poles in just two days. In another three days we put the poles into position. One of us would tie one end of the rope round his waist and the other end to the pole and haul it into position. Then we did the wiring. We all worked, including the *Harijans* and the children. The whole village worked. It became a pleasure. Within less than a month all the work had been completed. The Government would have taken six months may be.[1] We made the tube-wells in the existing wells. Some of them needed extra boring.

"When we first arrived we lived for some time in nearby villages with our relatives and friends. We came directly to this place because it was from this very neighbourhood about 60 years ago that our fathers migrated to colonize the new canal irrigated lands in West Punjab,[2] which we have had to leave now. Originally we belong to this district. Our relatives who had stayed behind then are still here."

Watan Singh, the oldest among them, with a very grey beard but a straight back, remembers the earlier emigration to the west clearly. He was old enough at the time to have helped his father in the field and to accompany him to the new land of promise.

"From Lahore we had to walk 50 miles", he recalls. "For the rest we rode on camels. There was no other mode of transport. The women had to be left behind, and for the first few years, I remember, we men had to grind the corn and cook our own food. We lopped off green branches from trees to make cots to sleep on." By the time the present generation was born, however, they had settled down to high prosperity.

"And now, a little over half a century later, I have had to trek back

---

[1] In addition to the saving on time, they also saved the government several thousand rupees.

[2] "The colony canals of the Punjab have been the most striking irrigational development of the period under review. Their primary object was not to serve areas already cultivated, but to make possible the colonization and development of the immense areas of waste crown land which existed in the province within recent years and on which large numbers of colonists selected from congested districts have since been settled on specific terms as lessees of the state. . . . Colonization began in 1892. . . . By 1901 the population of the tract had increased from practically nil to 800,000. . . . The headquarters of the colony are at Lyallpur, one of the most flourishing towns in Upper India." (*The Cambridge History of India*, Vol.VI, Cambridge, 1932, pp. 283-4).

exactly on the same route", says Watan Singh with a wry smile. "Who would have dreamed it?"

The name of the village is Edna Kalaska. The story is only one of thousands, about people similarly uprooted by the partition of India, and thereby of the Punjab (and Bengal) in August, 1947. More than half of this small village consists of flat-roofed mud huts. "We have now rebuilt a dozen of the *kutcha* houses and in addition eight new brick houses." These stand apart, brand new and modern in the rural context.

Atom and the Universe

The peasant in Uttar Pradesh, I have ventured to observe, is highly sophisticated, even if illiterate, and his thinking is usually in terms of the universe and the universal. Without ever stepping beyond the boundary of his village and its *mandi*, or at the utmost of the district town, he has an inborn genius for discovering the universe in the atom. The Punjabi, on the other hand, noticeably lacks any such philosophical sweep and agility of mind. However, if seized with the urge and curiosity, he will not hesitate to walk the universe in search of the atom. The characteristic tends to make him more mobile as well as more enterprising.

There is Pritaram, for instance, in a small village near Phillaur. He is a refugee from Lyallpur district. His father was an illiterate landless agricultural labourer, but "we were so hard up after partition that I decided to go away to England". He says it casually, as if England were next door, or at least nearer than Delhi. "Oh, I borrowed the money to pay for my fare, which I have returned already. Now I have purchased some land to build a house." In personal appearance also, Pritaram is totally transformed. He wears a black suit with a white shirt and sweater. While in London, "I did cloth business", he says, "as a peddler". He speaks English and has just returned having spent eight years abroad. Pritaram is a *Harijan*.

In the same neighbourhood there is Lachman Singh, a Sikh *Jat*, who has also returned from England only recently. Tall and handsome, he is a refugee from Dosan Kalan, a village in Lyallpur. In a shirt, sweater and a blue *tehmat* he explains: "I went abroad because I felt that by going I might be able to improve our economic condition. Unfortunately I developed asthma and so had to come back early. I went only to London. I worked there as a labourer." Inderjeet is another young man, in a pink turban. "My wife's father is in

Canada. I do not know exactly where." Inderjeet is waiting for the
father-in-law to call them over so that he also can cross the seas to
seek his fortune. He is eager to go.

"Everyone would like to go abroad—who wouldn't?" comments
Asa Ram, another *Harijan*, a casual agricultural labourer.

It is this attitude among the masses of the Punjab which allows for
greater economic flexibility and vocational mobility than the established orthodox social system within an Indian village generally per-
mits.

Crossing the "Line"

Thus, in villages everywhere it is still the normal practice for a
carpenter's son to become a carpenter, a weaver's son to become a
weaver, and a potter's son to become a potter, not only for practical
reasons, but because these professions are regulated by caste
unless the son goes to school and for long enough. Then alone he
qualifies to break through the caste custom of inheriting his profession, though it is usually only to seek a white-collar job of some
description.[1]

In a small village in Gurdaspur District, however, there lived an
ordinary blacksmith named Rattan Singh. Totally illiterate, he used
to manufacture locks, small brass ones and some big ones, and also
the bit for the horse's rein. Rattan Singh's clients were local landlords who paid him in kind. His house had one brick wall facing the
village lane; the others were all of mud. The entrance opened into a
yard where he did his work and beyond were a couple of small dark
rooms in which the family lived.

Rattan Singh had two sons. He did not send them to school. But
neither did he train them to become blacksmiths like himself, though
by prevailing standards business was good. Instead he advised the
boys, when they were ten and 14 years old, to go to Batala town, about
ten miles away, and learn what must, at the time, have been the latest
thing—"*saving*[2] machine repair work". He bought them, almost
from scrap, one bicycle costing twelve rupees, which would serve for
their transport. This was in 1922. Four years later when the
brothers decided to work on their own, their father gave them one
rupee and four annas to get started.

[1] Or an entirely new kind of job in a factory, for example, which does not fall
within any traditional occupational category of caste.

[2] Local pronunciation for "sewing".

Unable to buy a sewing machine or its parts with the capital at their disposal the two brothers initiated a business on the open pavement of a busy street. While one of them painted simple designs on small pieces of glass which are used for decorating bridal beds, the other purchased a tube of solution and a piece of rubber and offered to repair cycle punctures and earned three annas on the first day.

"The town did not have a single cycle repair shop in those days", they recall. There used to be only an enterprising gardener who repaired punctured tubes in his spare time at the house of the client. "Batala, of course was more like an overgrown village in those days. In 1926 it had seven bicycles in all. We can even tell you the names of the owners."

In 1959, the same town must have at least 70,000 bicycles on the road, and the two brothers have become the manufacturers of cycle rims of high quality which find a ready market as far away as Delhi and beyond. Rattan Singh, the village blacksmith, used to sell his locks for a handful of grain. The turnover of his sons' business is in the neighbourhood of 250,000 rupees per annum.

The Singh brothers live in Batala now in middle-class style, in double-storied houses which they have built themselves. By caste they continue to be blacksmiths, but not by profession. Their ancestral village is still there off the main Upper Bari Doab Canal. It is not very different from what it used to be in the 1920's. A car cannot enter its lanes, and it has the usual complement of children, goats, cowdung piles, dirt heaps, mud walls and a few brick houses. There are green fields of wheat and mustard; sturdy Sikh peasants are working in them. Flights of parakeets catch the winter sun on their wings. Rattan Singh's house is crumbling, empty.

There is also the more recent example of Wasan from a village in Amritsar District, who similarly crossed the "line". He went to Bhakra[1] about seven years ago, he says, and managed to get himself a job.

"I had never done this kind of work before. I'd been a farmer all my life; I have 60 *bighas* of land."

"Then why did you leave the village?" I ask.

"Oh, I have three brothers. They look after the land", he replies.

At Bhakra Wasan started as a driller on a monthly wage of 53

[1] Here the tallest high gravity dam in the world is being built across the river Sutlej, one of independent India's most ambitious hydel and irrigation projects.

rupees. "I learned quickly and now I am getting 158 rupees as a vibrator-operator. No one else from my village is working at Bhakra. I have brought my family here, since I have quarters to live in."

He saw big machines for the first time in Bhakra. He has never been to school, but he is ambitious. "I can understand the work of Bhakra", Wasan says confidently. "I can learn it. But they won't let me. They won't teach me. If they would make me a foreman I am sure I could do the job."

What is more, Wasan likes it at Bhakra. He says he has no friends or society of any kind. But "this work is better than agriculture", according to him. "I would prefer to get work like this elsewhere if I can, once this finishes."

"Why?"

"Here, for one thing, I get my pay regularly every month. It is not so in the village. Besides, I am happy, because I can live well here"— which is plainly visible from his outfit.

"I have kept my wife with me. Otherwise, how would I know what she does behind my back? She also is happier here. Now she has to cook only for one man. At home she would have to cook for a dozen. Here she has practically no work. Then, here the latrine is in the house. There my wife would have to get up before dawn and go out in the fields. Life in a village is very different. I do not want to go back to the village if I can help it", he repeats softly, his eyes to the ground.

Traditional Kinships

It is not that there is no orthodoxy, or traditional taboos, in the Punjab. To a man the Punjabi peasants are bitterly opposed to the recent reform enacted by the Indian Parliament relating to the Hindu law of inheritance,[1] whereby girls are now entitled to an equal share with boys in the family property. According to them, it will destroy the cordial relationship that exists normally between brothers and sisters, while actually few girls will benefit because they will be compelled, or "persuaded" rather, to "surrender voluntarily" their claims in the land at least. They feel that girls are given their due share by way of dowry in marriage. Nikka Singh in Fatehpur goes to

[1] "Hindu Succession Act" of 1956. Formerly, Hindu women were excluded from any right to a share in property, a practice now considered to be out of line with modern social trends and opposed to the principles of the Indian Constitution, which seeks to accord equality to both the sexes.

the extent of fearing that the law might revive the old custom of *dukhtar kushi*.[1]

"People who made this law do not have any sons", he says shaking his bearded face gravely. "They do not know what it means. Sons and daughters are not equal."

Similarly, in the village of Shamspur, at least 40 of its families have been affected adversely by the post-independence tenancy reforms.[2] They are no longer able to get any land on lease. White-bearded Khem Singh, for example, used to lease 50 *bighas*. Now he cannot get even one acre.

"Why did you not assert your legal right over the land you were cultivating when the reform came?" I enquire. "You knew you could not be thrown out, didn't you?"

"I do not ask or depend on the government for more land. God alone is the giver", replies Khem Singh. "Even without the 50 *bighas, langar lagda hai.*"[3]

"You see, in this village we are all descended from a single ancestor", explains Seva Singh, the *panchayat*'s president. "It is a very old village. Originally it belonged to a Pathan called Shamskhan. But he had no son. So he left it to Baba Wariam, from whom we are all descended. Therefore, even if one of us has cultivated the same piece of land for ten years continuously, he will not try to appropriate it, though he has the right to do so. Unless the owner gives it to him of his own accord, the lessee will not ask for it."

It is exactly as John Stuart Mill had reported to the House of Commons a hundred years ago, in 1857. In the Punjab, he states, "A village is not inhabited by a certain number of *Ryots* each unconnected with the other, but by a number of persons of common descent, forming one large cousinhood, having their own head man accustomed to joint action and mutual support."[4]

Where such bonds of traditional tribal kinship do not exist the attitude of the contracting parties is of course very different. Ratna Ram, for instance, a tenant from Bish, tried to assert his right over the 24 acres that he had been cultivating on lease in a neighbouring

---

[1] Killing of girls at birth. It was widely prevalent in the old days.

[2] "Punjab Security of Land Tenures (Amendment) Act", 1955.

[3] Food is cooked.

[4] Return to an Order of the House of Commons dated June 9, 1857, signed by John Stuart Mill, then Examiner of India Office correspondence, showing under what tenures, and subject to what Land Tax, lands were held under the several Presidencies of India. (Quoted in *The Economic History of India in the Victorian Age* by Romesh Dutt, Kegan Paul, London, 6th Ed., p. 96).

village. But Ratna Ram was given a sound beating, and there the matter ended.

Wells and Cowdung Cakes

In the case of Wasan, also, it was only in his village that I could discover the real reason for his reluctance to return home. For one thing, as it turned out, neither he nor his family own an inch of land. One of his brothers works for a landowner for a wage of 22 *maunds* of grain per annum plus his daily meals. The other two do casual labour and get through the year with difficulty. Together with their old mother, their wives and children, they live in stark poverty and filth in one-room mud huts, their clothes black with age, torn and patched, their faces pale and pinched with constant under-nourishment.

Theirs is a small village with only 105 houses. If Wasan had to return he would have to face not only the major economic problem of earning a sufficient livelihood and the minor inconvenience of his wife not having a latrine on the premises. He would also have to revert, professionally and socially, to the position to which he was born in the established social strata within the village, which in his case happens to be the lowliest even among the *Harijans*. Caste stratifications continue to be rigid within a village, and Wasan is a *Balmiki*. In Bhakra, secure in the anonymity of a vibrator-operator, he could sit on a sofa and have a cup of tea with me in the presence of his executive engineer.[1] In the village, while his wife may have to clean other people's latrines, he would not be permitted even to draw water to drink from any of the wells, except that of his own community.

Thus, in a village near Ambala, the *Jats* of the village had to give a separate well to the *Balmikis* because even the local *Ramdasis*, who are also *Harijans*[2] and who had a well of their own, would not permit the *Balmikis* to use it.

In the same village I walked into the house of a grey-bearded Sikh peasant. Though not too impressive or clean, his house is big. In the courtyard two beautiful big bullocks are standing with a bright yellow cloth covering their backs. Cotton is lying on the ground to dry. The man has sufficient land, and according to him everything is

---

[1] Even there it is not a normal occurrence, for different cadres and classes do not mix socially.

[2] *Balmikis* are the scavengers while *Ramdasis* are cobblers. *Balmikis* are rated lower than the *Ramdasis* in the caste hierarchy. *Jats* are the main peasant community of the Punjab.

fine. He is not a refugee and his fortunes therefore have not suffered any recent upheaval. Just then a woman comes in, wearing a blue *salwar* and *kameez*.[1] A warm shawl covers her head and part of the face. Slim, light of skin and with buck teeth and dirty hands she is obviously very angry. Mistaking me perhaps for an emissary of the government, she lets forth a torrent of complaints: not only is the present administration not doing anything for the *zemindars*,[2] but it is positively conspiring against them.

"But why are you so angry?" I ask mildly as soon as I can get in a word.

"Why?" she repeats. "The government has given land to *Harijans* in this village. The result is that they will not do our work.[3] And now I, a *Jat* woman" (with heavy emphasis on the word *Jat*) "I have to dirty my hands and do this work of making cowdung cakes. Is this a *Jat's* work?"

"But don't you want the condition of *Harijans* also to improve?" I ask.

"Why should it?" is the forceful reply with the full weight of conviction behind it. "*Harijans* were born to do menial jobs. God made them such, and they should be allowed to continue as such. Am I meant for this—do I deserve it?" and she holds out her dirty hands to invite sympathy.[4]

[1] The Punjabi women's dress of baggy trousers and a long shirt.
[2] Meaning simply landowners in this case. There were no *zemindars* in the Punjab as in Bihar and Uttar Pradesh. This has always been a *ryotwari* area of peasant proprietors, as, for example, in Tanjore. But it is interesting to note that, although the tenancy system is the same in these two regions, the attitude to work and pattern of working are strikingly different. Thus, whereas the bulk of farm work in Tanjore (and in Madras) is done through hired labour, it is exactly the opposite in the Punjab. The percentage of agricultural labour families in the Punjab is only 10·1 as against 53 in Madras, while the cultivating classes (both landowners and tenants) in the Punjab constitute 61·2 per cent, as against 26·7 per cent in Madras. (Based on *1951 Census* and *Reports of All India Agricultural Labour Enquiry, 1950–51*).
[3] Three years ago *Harijan* families here were formed into a co-operative society and given 35 acres of government land for cultivation. Actually the co-operative is not working as such, and each member is farming his own piece of land separately. But apparently the *Harijans* have stopped doing casual labour since they have their own lands to cultivate now.
[4] But whereas at least this woman does make the cowdung cakes, however reluctantly, in many upper caste villages in Western Uttar Pradesh I found compost pits, dug at the instance of government officials, lying empty and the refuse meant to go into them piled up instead in heaps at the entrance to the village, simply because the higher castes will not handle the refuse themselves. A *bhangin* is engaged to do the job, but she cannot be persuaded to take it further than the outskirts of the village, where she throws it on a pile, a separate one for each household. Most of the compost pits are at a distance, in the fields, and they remain empty.

(Continued on next page)

This refusal to handle the compost ingredients, rooted in caste custom and tradition, persists despite the government having appointed in many areas special "compost" extension officers to ensure that the peasants make good farmyard manure. Many villages in the Punjab, and in other States as well, face the same problem for the same reason and are unable to solve it.

As the peasants of Ghaloli, near Saharanpur, in Western UP, said to me: "To our shame we have to admit that we do not make good quality compost simply because our lands are at some distance from the village and the *bhangin* will not carry the refuse so far. She simply throws it in a heap near the road and the rain washes away most of it."

It is not that the peasants of Ghaloli are ignorant of or unfamiliar with the technique of making good compost. And they fully appreciate its value as manure. In fact, on *Diwali* day, just as they worship all other valuables, so a *diva* is lit on the garbage heap also.

CHAPTER XIV

DYNAMICS OF CHANGE

As an instrument of change in patterns of human behaviour the power of pure reason by itself is perhaps rarely effective. In the Punjab, certainly, more than reason or persuasion compulsions of history, and especially the recent partition of the State, seem to have played a vital role in weakening traditional trammels and taboos, especially those which restrict the choice and nature of a man's work.

The Punjab has borne the brunt and the first impact of almost all the major invasions by foreign powers from time immemorial, this having been the traditional route of entry into the sub-continent.[1] The result has been that the people of the Punjab have developed an unusual capacity for adjustment to change, which makes them one of the least "rooted" communities in India, mentally, culturally and physically. Not only are traces of Muslim culture strongest in the Punjab, both among the Hindus and the Sikhs, but also it is the Punjabi today, at all levels of society, who aspires, perhaps more than any other, to what is loosely termed the western culture and manner of living. Every village and hamlet here bears witness to it. This is true even though the British advanced into the country from the south and the east and Punjab was the last to be annexed, only in the 1840's.[2]

Then in the holocaust of 1947, within a period of about four months, the Hindu and Sikh population in the western districts of the State had to flee on a scale and in circumstances too well known to

---

[1] Only the very last arrivals, the Europeans, came by sea.

[2] Another reason for this is the fact that under British rule Punjabis were given preference in recruitment to the Indian Army. It would be difficult to find a peasant family in the State from which one or more men have not served in the armed forces and been abroad in consequence. The experience naturally widened their horizons considerably.

need recounting.[1] Not only were millions suddenly uprooted from the security of their homes, but there was a considerable disparity between their occupational pattern and that of the Muslim evacuees to Pakistan whom they replaced. The immigrants, therefore, could not be absorbed easily in the vacuum left by the Muslims, and for sheer survival were often compelled to change their trades or at least the pattern of their working.

Batala, for example, has long been an industrial centre and was especially known for the manufacture of simple agricultural implements. The town has an incredible air of bustle and noise; there is a constant din of hammers and electric motors, while the pavements are littered with trunks, brass utensils, scrap, furniture and packing cases. Till 1947, however, almost all its factories were owned by Muslims and the workmen also were nearly all Muslims. Hindus in the town were mainly money-lenders and shopkeepers.[2]

Now it would be difficult to find a Muslim in Batala. The entire manufacturing business there, as in the rest of the State in fact, has been taken over and greatly expanded and improved upon by the Hindu and Sikh immigrants, almost none of whom had ever done this kind of work before.

In the cycle rim factory of the Singh brothers, for instance, out of 40 workmen all but three are refugees, none of whom had ever handled a machine before the partition. Mostly illiterate, they are drawn from various low castes such as tanners, potters, barbers and other Scheduled Castes. But for the partition they would still be the landless elements in their villages, pursuing their respective traditional caste trades or working simply as agricultural labourers.

A typical foundry establishment, also in Batala, was, till 1947, a Muslim concern with all Muslim workmen. It manufactured simple chaff-cutters. After the partition it was allotted to a Hindu refugee, and the plant now employs 48 people, almost all of whom are immigrants and completely new to the work. Moreover, instead of chaff-cutters, the foundry has started producing the much more complicated lathe machines. It is now scheduled also to make grinding machines—"of as good a quality as Hindustan Machine Tools

---

[1] According to the 1951 census, 2,731,929 immigrants from Pakistan settled in the Punjab (I). Of these 1,276,827 or 46·7 per cent were agriculturists. The total population of Punjab is 16,100,000 in an area of 47,334 square miles.

[2] In the rural areas, also, whereas the Hindus and Sikhs were mainly the peasantry in east Punjab in pre-partition days, the Muslims were the artisans.

H

Factory[1] in Bangalore". On its staff, however, the foundry has three pattern-makers, who are responsible for making patterns for castings, but they cannot read a drawing or even figures, being totally illiterate. Simple carpenters before, they have never used micrometers or any precision instruments and are reluctant to use them now.

Vaishnodas, who is in charge of the workshop in the foundry, came from Narowal in Pakistan. Though he had studied up to the sixth class, he had never handled a machine before. His father was a trader in rice. The supervisor of the foundry, Dayal Singh, never went to school and is totally illiterate. His father was a goldsmith.

The change-over was not very drastic for the landowning agriculturists among the refugees, because ultimately they were all able to get at least some land in exchange to cultivate, though not as much[2] or always of as good quality as they had in West Punjab. Even in their case, however, most of the large landlords were accustomed to having their lands in West Punjab tilled by Muslim tenants while they simply collected rent and perhaps did some other subsidiary business as well. Many of them have become now real owner-cultivators and are farming themselves for the first time. Before 1947 these very eastern districts of the Punjab were deficient in food production by about 35,000 tons; in less than ten years they have a handsome surplus. Moreover, despite the presence of nearly 3 million refugees, there is in the villages here practically none of the stark poverty and semi-starvation which has been such a striking feature almost everywhere else in the country.

It is significant, however, that from all accounts it is the immigrant peasant who is today generally more progressive and superior in husbandry and in techniques of cultivation to the native farmer of east Punjab—even in the case of the refugee who belongs to the same stock as the latter, and is only the first-generation descendant of the pioneers who had earlier migrated from these very districts to people the canal colonies in the West.[3] It would seem, therefore, that even within a historically "uprooted" people it is the "more uprooted" element that is comparatively more receptive to new ideas, more

[1] A government enterprise, employing the latest techniques and equipment in collaboration with a Swiss firm.

[2] A total of 4,735,310 acres was left by evacuee Muslim agriculturists in eastern Punjab, as against 6,729,050 left by the Hindus and Sikhs in Pakistan. This gap was covered by imposing graded cuts when making the allotments.

[3] The main body of the migrants to West Punjab had gone from the districts of Jullundur and Hoshiarpur, in east Punjab, the fertile Doaba as it is known, because of heavy pressure on land.

ambitious and hard working. As Karl Mannheim has stated, "up-rooting" has its positive aspects for personality formation. "Up-rooting, viewed positively, might be called emancipation."[1]

[1] *Freedom Power and Democratic Planning*, Kegan Paul, 1951, p. 63.
And yet it is not invariably so. The Bengali refugee of the 1947 partition did not show the same sturdy self-reliance, capacity for adjustment, hard work and spirit of adventure as the Punjabi. A possible reason could be that his earlier background was completely different and much more settled.

RAJASTHAN

CHAPTER XV

TINSEL AND TRACTORS

NOT only in the Punjab have the descendants of the "uprooted" pioneers of the canal colonies of Lyallpur and other western districts of that State proved to be highly enterprising. A good number of those early colonizers migrated again further south into the heart of the inhospitable desert of Rajasthan, where another canal system[1] reached out to irrigate nearly 1,000 square miles of the most barren and arid sands in the then State of Bikaner, and helped to develop it.

Water flowed through these channels for the first time on 26th October 1927 and brought into existence entirely new colonies with Shri Ganganagar, a new township, as their *mandi*[2] and district headquarters. Five hundred new villages were created in what came to be known as the Gang Canal area, and its population increased from a bare 28,000 in 1927 to 180,000 in 1934.[3] Almost all the immigrants were from the canal colonies of West Punjab. Now not only are the barren desert sands buried under lush green fields, but the district has become virtually the granary of Rajasthan.

In Thirty Years

"When I came 30 years ago there was not even a village here. I brought a tent and lived in it for six months. Then I made a small hut in the midst of my fields—just one small room. I did not bring my family, but kept a servant to cook my meals", recalls Sardar Teja Singh of *Chak* 3G.[4] "The landscape was so barren that we used to

---

[1] Under the Sutlej Valley Scheme.

[2] Grain marketing centre.

[3] According to 1951 census the population of Ganganagar District is 539,000 rural and 91,000 urban.

[4] The new settlements have no names. They were given numbers. "Chak" means village.

have to fix on a tree as a landmark to guide us. Otherwise we would lose our way. The *andheri* used to blow for days together, and it was impossible even to cook while it was blowing.[1] Now we do not get such sandstorms."

Fair of skin, with a greying beard, Teja Singh wears a green shirt, *tehmat* and a yellow turban. He is from Sargoda. "My father came originally from Ludhiana. He was a *Risaldar*[2] in the army and was given land in Sargoda. But since I have an elder brother, father bought me another 15 *morabbas*[3] here. The people who were living here originally, before the canals came, are the local Bagdis. They did not even know how to use the canal water. It was virgin land, though this soil is not as fertile as that of Sargoda and Lyallpur", says Teja Singh, shaking his finger. "Here we have to use fertilizer. Even then the yield of wheat is only 22 *maunds* an acre."

He first brought his land under the plough with bullocks and camels. Now he has a Fordson tractor and he has just bought "a new contraption" which also does harvesting, threshing and winnowing. His family operate the tractor themselves, rather than employ a driver. He is now thinking of buying a car.

"Oh, my father had to face the same kind of difficulties as I had to face here. At first he also lived in a tent and each day went on horse-back to work on the land. Then gradually he built his house, and so on."

Now, Teja Singh has his house in the village—a big modern brick building, well furnished. There are upholstered chairs in the living room, and a radio set; in the dining room, a table and chairs; lunch is served on china plates. The village does not have even a primary school, but Teja Singh has a daughter at college in the Punjab, and of his four sons, one is studying law, one runs a petrol pump, one is

---

[1] Francisco Pelsaert, a Dutchman, travelling in Upper India some 300 years ago describes such a sandstorm most vividly: "The air is filled with the dust raised by violent whirlwinds from the sandy soil, making day like the darkest night that human eyes have seen or that can be grasped by the imagination. Thus in the afternoon of 15 June, 1624, I watched a hurricane of dust coming up gradually, which so hid the sky and the sun that for two hours people could not tell if the world was at an end, for the darkness and fury of the wind could not have been exceeded"—Pelsaert, *Jehangir's India*, pp. 47–48; quoted in *The Cambridge History of India*, Vol. VI, Cambridge, 1932, p. 294.

[2] A *Risaldar* is a non-commissioned officer in the Indian Army. It was a policy of the British Government to give land in the canal colonies to men who served in the army. Ludhiana is in East Punjab, while Sargoda is in West Punjab in the canal area.

[3] One *morabba* = 15·6 acres.

in the United States, and one, Nirmal Singh, in khaki trousers and a green shirt, is managing the farm. Nirmal Singh is contesting the coming election for the presidency of the village *panchayat*; he says the contest will cost him 8,000 to 10,000 rupees.

Professional Cultivators

In another *chak* near by is Narendra Singh's house—also of brick, and of modern design. The living room has a beautiful carpet, double curtains, a sofa set. He himself is young and speaks fluent English. Narendra Singh's father also had canal land in Sargoda. His grandfather purchased these 13 *morabbas* here in 1928–29.

"Until 1947 tenants were cultivating this land. We came here after partition", Narendra Singh explains. A college graduate, he now devotes his entire time to the farm and has ten *morabbas* under cultivation. He owns a tractor, which he drives himself. He also has a jeep. His average yield of wheat is 23 *maunds* to an acre. It is the average for the whole village, all of whose residents are also Sikh *Jats* from Sargoda.

Narendra Singh is highly perturbed about the State's land policy and the proposed ceiling on holdings. On present calculations, he says, he will be allowed barely 15 acres to himself.

"We will have to leave farming and go", he says, stretching out both his hands and shrugging his shoulders. "But where can we go, that's the question. They want to make us into *ghasiaras*,[1] it seems. How can we maintain a decent standard of life on 15 acres?"

According to Narendra Singh, it is a grave mistake on the part of the administration to allot land to non-professional cultivators. "Many *Jagirdars*[2] from Udaipur and Kutch have been given canal-irrigated lands here. But they have not even bothered to come and live here. They have never done any cultivation themselves. How can they ever be good farmers?" he asks. "Only those who work themselves and understand agriculture should be given land. But the government is giving it to any and everybody."

Narendra Singh believes that the Sikh *Jats* of Majha and Doaba[3]

[1] Literal meaning: grass-cutters. Used in the sense of a "menial". All landowners, including the local Bagdis, have the same complaint of course.

[2] Some 2,476 ex-*Jagirdars* had been allotted land in canal areas up to the end of December 1958. *Jagirdars* in Rajasthan were like the *Jagirdars* in Hyderabad, feudal tax-farmers who did not themselves cultivate the land. With land reforms they also have lost their tax-farming rights. Seven to eight million acres of land is lying uncultivated in Rajasthan for want of cultivators.

[3] In the Punjab.

"have left everyone else in India far behind in agriculture. There are only three things a Punjabi can do; business, agriculture and soldiering. Of these, business used to be the monopoly of *Bhapas* of Rawalpindi district, while we have always been the best in agriculture. You cannot compare us with the local Bagdis; there is no comparison. This region, as you are perhaps aware, is known for its high consumption of fertilizer and improved seeds[1]—it is the highest in Rajasthan. But the highest consumption will be found in the Sikh *chaks*.

"With us", continues Narendra Singh earnestly, "if we see a better crop we must find out how it is so and why, and we will try out the new method and technique for ourselves. We will experiment. A Bagdi *chak*, on the other hand, will not cultivate sugar cane even though it pays much more, because Bagdis are afraid of the labour it requires and the fact that it takes a whole year to mature. They still grow mostly *bajra* and *jowar* because they are the easiest to cultivate. Their average yields of wheat, or any crop, will be less than half what we get."

A Bagdi Village

"No, we do not cultivate sugar cane, very little of it. You see, the return is too little, and then it takes a whole year to mature", says Khetpal. "On wheat our average yield is at the most ten *maunds* per acre."

"But it is no use applying fertilizer to our sandy soil", says Ratnaramji, shaking his head vigorously. He sits covered with a blanket on a *pidha*.[2] Ruparam concurs with Ratnaramji. "Our land is weak; it is all sand. It cannot take any fertilizer." All the assembled heads nod in agreement.

This village too is in the Gang Canal area, in the same neighbourhood as the two Punjabi *chaks* of Teja Singh and Narendra Singh. It has the same soil, the same climatic conditions, and it also first received canal irrigation in 1927, though the village itself is older. But this village is populated entirely by the local Bagdis. It has no Punjabi immigrants.

"It was the Punjabis who taught us how to cultivate with irrigation", continues Khetpal. "We did not know how to prepare the

---

[1] It probably also has the largest number of tractors and jeeps of any district in India.

[2] A low square seat of traditional design on four legs and strung with tape or strings, usually backless. It is widely in use in north Indian homes.

land and the beds and so on. It was also they who introduced cotton
and sugar cane in this area."

After 30 years of close association with the Punjabis, however,
these Bagdi cultivators still do not believe in using much fertilizer or
in cultivating more of commercial crops like sugar cane. Their
average yield of wheat is only ten *maunds* per acre. Moreover, no
man in the village, they say, ever bothers to take the advice or help of
the government agricultural extension officials in order to improve
his production.

Deva Ram, president of the village *panchayat*, a thin man with a
long nose and a not-too-fierce moustache, purchased a tractor recently, but he has sold it and gone back to ploughing with bullocks.
He found the tractor too expensive because he hired a driver to
operate it, and then "the oil is so costly." Khetpal also has a tractor
and he too engages a driver for it, to whom he pays 100 rupees per
month plus meals. They will not drive the tractors themselves.

Not only do the techniques of cultivation in their case thus remain
essentially traditional, but also the pattern of their consumption
and investment. Their income continues to be spent largely "on
our women, on their clothes and the tinsel which is used to decorate
them" admits Khetpal with a smile. Bagdi women here wear the
very full skirts, bone or ivory bangles to the elbow, and much
jewellery.[1] "Also, marriage expenses have increased. A jeep and
tractor are now added to the gold we have to give in dowry—oh,
purely as a matter of fashion. Whatever it be, it is always more than
one's capacity. Everyone in this village is in debt"—despite the
tremendous increase in their incomes since the canals came[2] and the
high prices they have been getting for their produce during most of
the two decades since World War II began.

We sit on the *chabutra* of the house of the richest man of the *chak*,
on string cots, *pidhas* and one solitary cane chair with a worn-out
leather covering. Many sit on the ground. The house is of traditional
design, as are all the rest. Only two or three structures in the whole
village have even a front wall of brick; not one house is constructed
entirely of brick. The children are in torn and dirty clothes, the men
in turbans and dirty *dhoties*. And yet nearly 50 families in this village

---

[1] Each skirt takes anything from ten to 25 yards of material; ivory bangles are also
very costly.

[2] As in Tanjore (Madras), here also the increase in their incomes is due primarily
to irrigation and not to harder work or the use of more scientific techniques of
cultivation.

own more than 50 acres each of canal-irrigated land. There is also a middle school with nearly 200 students.

"Before the canals came", recalls Khetpal, "even our drinking water had to be brought daily from a distance of 12 miles on camel back."

"In those days", continues Tansukh Ram, a white-bearded patriarch of 60, "if a man used more than one and a quarter *seers* of water in a day he believed that God would take an account from him after death and rebuke him for wasting so much water. One and a quarter *seers* had to suffice for bathing and everything. When it rained we got a meagre crop of *bajra*, *moth* and *til*. When the rains failed we would go to the *bund* and work as coolies carrying baskets of earth on our heads. We used to eat only barley or *bajra*.

"Now", and Tansukh Ram's eyes light up as, with a broad smile, he looks round for confirmation, "everyone among us eats wheat—yes, everyone."

Lakhonwali

The status value of wheat in these parts is very similar to that of rice in Tanjore and Coimbatore, and it could be of course that the horizons of the Bagdis here are similarly limited—to the ambition of eating wheat, and no more. Their progress in the past three decades since the canals came should in fairness be compared not with that of their more ambitious Punjabi immigrant neighbours, but with their own kind, who do not yet have the benefit of any irrigation facilities and whose level of existence now is much the same as it used to be for Khetpal, Tansukh Ram, Deva Ram and others 30 years ago.

In Lakhonwali, for example—"Not a single man eats wheat in this village", says Khuda Baksh, shaking his head. "No. Not even the richest man. He also eats *bajra*. We eat *jowar*, *bajra*, *makki*, *moth*, *chana*—whatever is available. But never wheat."

Lakhonwali is also in Bikaner division. But no branch of the Gang Canal comes this way. All around it are sand dunes, dazzling in the sunlight. The village has about 200 houses, in design and outward appearance exactly like those of Khetpal's village. But the latter has at least two or three structures with a brick frontage, while in Lakhonwali only one house, under construction now, has its outer wall facing the street in brick. The rest are all of mud.

Every family in Lakhonwali owns land. They have fairly large holdings. But there is not a tractor or jeep in the village, only the loose-jointed camel.

Vegetation here is limited to small shrubs, thorny and black. Even the grass is black. The few patches of cultivation have in their midst small mounds of sand, while the crops themselves look like a week's growth on an unshaven chin. Average yields here are one *maund* of *jowar* or *bajra* per *bigha*, sometimes less. They cannot cultivate wheat or sugar cane.

Their greatest problem, of course, is water. Average rainfall is eight inches per annum. They collect the rain in a pond but it lasts only for two months. For the rest of the year water has to be carted in on camel-back from Rawatsar, six miles away.

"I was born and bred here," says Subhan, one of the peasants. About 60 years of age, he has a gentle face, with a small, white beard trimmed to a point and round, tin-framed spectacles tied to the ear on one side with a black thread. "When I was young there was no well in the village. This one was made 50 years ago; it succeeded only at the fifth attempt, I remember. But its water is drinkable in winter only, if mixed with sweet water. If we take it in summer, it causes diarrhoea."

The well is probably the only memorable development the village has known in 50 years. It still has no school, and only one brave boy from Lakhonwali, Farida's ten-year-old son Allahbux, daily walks the five miles to and from the school in Ranjitpura.

CHAPTER XVI

CHANNELS OF COMMUNICATION

THE residents of Lakhonwali, however, are looking forward to better times. Outside the village in the midst of the yellow sands, red flags flutter on posts to mark the route of another canal, the Rajasthan Canal, which will be the longest irrigation channel in the world. When completed it will irrigate 2·6 million acres of arid desert sand.[1] This region too will then become green and fertile like the Ganganagar district, and the peasants of Lakhonwali also will be able to eat wheat instead of the cheaper millets they now consume. They are very happy at the prospect.

"We heard that Nehrulal[2] came to Tibbi, and with a gold *karandi* and *kudal* laid two bricks to inaugurate the canal", says Khuda Baksh. "Nehrulal—the Pandit, who does good works", he explains further, in case I do not know to whom he is referring.

Not one man from Lakhonwali, however, bothered to go to Tibbi, only 20 miles away, to witness the inauguration of a project which will completely transform the economy and life of its whole population. "No, no one went from the village", says Khuda Baksh. "Nor do we know where the canal will go or anything. We only know it is coming here."

Neither have they heard about the Five Year Plans under which the Rajasthan Canal is being constructed. In fact, they have practically no information about anything in the outside world, except Nehru. Even him they have never seen, but as Subhan expressed it: "We have heard he is very good. He is our *mai-bap*.[3] We know of no other benefactor."

[1] It will take off from the Harike Barrage, just below the confluence of the Sutlej and Beas rivers in the Punjab, and end in Ramgarh, a tiny hamlet west of Jaisalmer in Rajasthan, its length totalling 425 miles.

[2] Actually, the late Govind Ballabh Pant, the Union Home Minister, had been to Tibbi and not Nehru.

[3] Literal translation: "mother-father"

The isolation of Lakhonwali is by no means exceptional. The village of Nichalgarh,[1] for example, got a road six years ago. But the village acquired its first bullock cart only two months back. There is not yet a bicycle in this village. The terrain here is suited for it, but as the peasants Lalajala and Uda Deva put it: "We do not know how to ride it, so what would be the use of getting it. We cannot have a driver for the cycle as you have for your cars and we will break our bones if we fall trying to learn it." They are both young Girasiyas, with dark but sharp features and extremely white teeth of perfect formation.[2]

A Man or a Woman?

In the first fortnight of January 1959, at Nagpur, the Indian National Congress held its annual session, in itself an important event every year. At this particular session, moreover, the conference adopted certain weighty policy resolutions on agrarian reforms to serve as directives to the governments in the States and at the Centre. In view of the hitherto unsatisfactory progress in the field of agricultural production, it recommended speedy implementation of tenancy reforms, early enactment of ceiling legislation, and adoption of joint farming as the future pattern of farm organization. It also advised the immediate establishment of rural service co-operatives of various kinds in all villages.

These decisions should have been of intimate concern to every farmer in India, for when implemented they would alter radically not only his economic prospects but also the pattern of his work for generations to come. The pronouncements made headlines in the entire Indian press, and though they provoked a good deal of controversy the Nagpur Conference was acclaimed as historic. But though it is February now, a month after the Nagpur Session, none of the peasants I meet in Rajasthan, barring a few educated middle-class Sikh cultivators in Shri Ganganagar, appear to have heard of the resolutions yet, or even that the ruling party had held a conference.[3]

---

[1] In Sirohi district. The village is inhabited mainly by Girasiyas and seven families of Pathans.

[2] The case of Nichalgarh is exceptional. Cycles are very common now in most villages in India which have roads and are fairly near a town.

[3] This despite the fact that under a directive of the Congress, party members had just completed *pad yatras* (walking tours) throughout the country, to contact the rural masses and inform them about the decisions taken at the Nagpur Conference.

In Daba,[1] for instance, a highly prosperous village of 160 families, even though its young *panch* is a member of the local Mandal Committee of the Congress, neither he nor any one else in the village has heard of the recent Congress Session or of the Five Year Plan.

It is the same in Kalwad, although this village is only 16 miles distant from the State capital at Jaipur. Set against a background of a ring of low hills littered with stones and small thorny shrubs, Kalwad is a big village and a highly "developed" one: it has 250 irrigation wells, a school building, a tanning and weaving centre, an *ambar charkha* training centre and a credit co-operative society. The latter co-exists with a formidable looking money-lender with heavy gold earrings, to whom most of the villagers are duly indebted. The village is building a *panchayat ghar* and within a year will have a primary health centre. It also has a school with five teachers and 150 pupils, a library, and two wireless sets, one of which belongs to the *panchayat*. Even so, none of them has heard of the Congress session at Nagpur. No one reads a newspaper,[2] and apparently neither of the radios is working.

In Bhoola, a Bhil village in Sirohi district, the villagers admit: "Yes, we have heard of the Congress. We have heard of the Congress; yes. Everyone talks of it."

"But", pauses Kania, gravely puckering his bushy eyebrows, "but now that you mention it, we do not know whether Congress is a man or a woman."

---

[1] In Nokha Block, Bikaner Division, a village consisting mainly of *Rajputs, Jats, Kumhars* and *Harijans*. Every family has land, including the *Harijans*. The average holding is 100 *bighas*. Like most peasants in these semi-arid areas, they also trade in wool and livestock and actually are better off economically than most of their counterparts in the "wet" regions of Rajasthan.

[2] Except for one paralytic patient who is a matriculate; but it seems no one else benefits from it. It is not only in the sandy tracts of Rajasthan, however, that there is still such meagre communication of ideas and information. Barring small pockets like Kerala, absence of communication is a conspicuous feature of most of the rural landscape everywhere in India, despite the tremendous improvement of late in the means and modes of transport. As already noted, in the Punjab there is greater mobility and alertness among the peasants than elsewhere and far fewer preservatives of antiquities, such as sand or tradition. But even in the Punjab none of the peasants I met during my tour had heard of the Congress session at Nagpur and of its momentous resolutions, though it was just after the conference had ended. They had not heard of it even in villages with high schools, community radio sets, government Information Centres, and several literates, villages such as Nanheri, Shamspur, Mallehwal and Fatehpur, to name just a few. Apparently, the villagers neither read newspapers nor listen to the news, even if the radio is in working order, as it normally is only if it is privately owned.

They Will Not Go To Delhi

Until only a decade ago, of course, Bhoola, Kalwad, Daba, Lakhon-wali were all in Indian princely States,[1] where there was no Congress nor for that matter any political party. In any case the Congress, the oldest of the existing political parties in India, is less than three-quarters of a century old, while many of the erstwhile ruling *Rajput* families here trace their lineage in unbroken descent as far back as the pre-Christian era. Much older traditions therefore still hold their sway, and time seems to have stood still through the centuries in many parts of Rajasthan.

There are a dozen villages on Mt. Abu, for instance, whose residents are forbidden to descend to the plains below even to marry. Abu itself is at the southern end of the Aravalli range,[2] which cuts across Rajasthan diagonally from south-west to north-east for about 300 miles. Separated somewhat from the main range, it is a single peak surrounded by the plains. The tradition against going down, which some of Abu's peasants still observe, must come from the times when Rajput clans were being hunted relentlessly by the Moghal armies, and the Aravalli range was their only friend and shelter.

For a quarter of a century when Rana Pratap fought the might of Akbar's empire, he commanded his subjects, on pain of death, to retire into the mountains.[3] The injunction continues to be obeyed to this day, four centuries later, so that not a single man from Salgaon, for instance, one of the dozen such villages, has ever been anywhere beyond or rather below Mt. Abu.

In the plains below Abu, on the other hand, there is a widespread legend that anyone who goes to Delhi, especially the women, will never return. Just two years ago, when the government wanted to take a folk dance group from the Pindwara Block to participate in the folk dances of the annual Republic Day celebrations in the capital,

---

[1] Until independence, Rajputana, as it was then called, consisted of a conglomeration of some 25 princely States and Chiefships. These were integrated in several stages, and the State of Rajasthan as it is today emerged only on 1st November, 1956, with an area of 132,152 square miles and a population of roughly 16 million.

[2] To the east of the Aravalli range lies the more fertile region of the State and to ts west the great Indian desert.

[3] From 1572 to 1597. Apart from protection the idea was also to reduce the rich plains of Mewar to desolation so that they should be of no value to the conqueror.

to a man (and woman) they refused. Only with the greatest difficulty were they finally persuaded to agree.[1]

In Jolliali,[2] according to the villagers themselves, their life in practically every detail—dress, housing, food, beliefs—continues to be, almost exactly as it was two and a half centuries ago when the village was founded. One of the peasants, Jalluram, with a small moustache and gold earrings, holds that, "Perhaps the main difference since 1947 is that we have lost our fear. If we see a police constable or a district official now we are not afraid of him as we used to be." But within the village they continue to observe strictly all the traditional rituals and orthodoxies.[3] There is little or no revolt or non-conformism among the younger generation, either.

Thus, only a month ago in a neighbouring hamlet a peasant spent 13,000 rupees on a *moser* or death feast. "Eighty *maunds* of *halwa*[4] was prepared for which alone 80 tins of pure *ghee*[5] were used! If a man does not give the death feast he will be taunted by the neighbours that they saw the spirit of the dead sitting on the tree, and so on," explains Kolaram Baba, the most prosperous man in the village and the picture of antiquity in his beautiful beard, *angarkha*, *dhoti* and turban.

"And please do not tell our women about all these rights and strange new notions of equality that you mention"[6], the Baba pleads with me. "Our woman is taught not to worship Ram even—only the husband. She must devote all her time to serve him; only then can she hope to earn her salvation."

[1] The same story was repeated a year later in Jodhpur district, where the villagers believed in the same legend and just as strongly. The belief undoubtedly goes back to the sixteenth century, to the time of Akbar, who had instituted a special festival of *nauroza* when the wives of the *Rajput* vassal princes were congregated at the court of the Moghal Emperor, and according to James Tod, "*Rajput* honour was bartered, and . . . many of the noblest of the race were dishonoured."—Lieut. Col. James Tod, *Annals and Antiquities of Rajasthan*, Humphrey Milford, Vol. I, pp. 399–400.

[2] Twenty-five miles from Jodhpur. Here the average rainfall is 14 inches per annum. The village has approximately 200 houses and every family has land. The average holding is about 60 *bighas*. But it is a single crop area and entirely rain fed. The main income of the peasants comes from trading in livestock, dairy products and wool.

[3] The inhabitants are a sect of *Bishnois*. They worship Jambojeedata, hold the deer as sacred, are strict vegetarians and will not eat food cooked by anyone but themselves, not even a *Brahmin*. Even in the desert they must bathe first thing in the morning. They never dance and they bury their dead.

[4] A sweet preparation. As a Minister of the State remarked, "the money spent on these death and marriage feasts in Rajasthan would suffice to finance its Five Year Plans." Restrictions have since been imposed on death feasts by an act of legislation.

[5] Clarified butter costing Rs.105 per tin.

[6] The laws recently passed by the Indian Parliament giving Hindu girls the right of inheritance and the right of divorce, about which these villagers heard for the first time from me and were duly shocked.

NEFA

CHAPTER XVII

IN THE LAND OF THE TRIBES

"WE are very eager now to have a road to Dibrugarh", says Binsen Lollen. "We want to get out and see the world. At present we can reach only Along. We do not know what Hindustan is. We say *Jai Hind* because we have been taught to. But we do not even know its meaning. They refer to Congress *raj* but we have never seen a Congressman. We have heard of Jawaharlal Mehru [sic] but never seen him."

Binsen Lollen is a village leader in Kombong, a village in Siang Frontier Division of the distant North East Frontier Agency.[1] On the extremity of the Indian boundary, NEFA is one of the most isolated tracts in India, inhabited entirely by a tribal population of 600,000, which is ethnically Indo-Mongoloid and is divided between 50 language groups, inclusive of dialects.[2]

Over 30,000 square miles in area, hardly any of it flat, NEFA adjoins Bhutan to the west, Tibet and the Sikang regions of China to the north and east, and Burma to the south-east. Though constitutionally a part of the State of Assam, it is administered directly by the Central Government's Ministry of External Affairs, with the Governor of Assam acting as the Agent of the President of India.

India has a large tribal population—the largest of any country in the world perhaps—estimated to number nearly 23 million people. Not only do their cultural and social structures differ greatly from those prevalent among "non-tribal" communities in India, but also there are wide variations among the different tribes themselves, even within NEFA. Thus, the Sherdukpens and Akas of Kameng

[1] Some of the background information for this section is drawn from Verrier Elwin's *A Philosophy for NEFA*, Shillong, 1959. The author is a noted anthropologist and adviser to the Government of India on tribal affairs.

[2] Few of the languages of these tribals are written, and they belong to the Tibeto-Burman branch of the main Sino-Tibetan family.

Division are dominated by an aristocratic class which is still very powerful. The Daflas and Mishamis regard the family rather than the village as the unit of society, so theirs is a highly individualistic community. The Apa Tanis have a strong sense of private possession, since they have long been practising settled, as opposed to shifting, cultivation; in their case, influence and social status is associated mainly with landed property. The Monpas of Kameng and Khamptis of Lohit Frontier Division are Buddhists. The Khamptis especially, who immigrated from the Shan States of Burma towards the end of the eighteenth century, are highly sophisticated. Then there are the Noctes, who have adopted a very elementary form of Vaishnaivism, and the virile Wanchoos—both till recently head hunters. One can still see bracket-loads of human skulls in their village *Morung*[1] preserved as trophies. They have the chieftain system, under which chiefs are paid tribute by the villages. They have three social classes —the chiefs, the "proletariat" and an intermediate class—and they do not intermarry.

Consequently, the approach to the socio-economic problems of the tribals must be different in each case, and the pattern of development adapted to the special needs, social conditions and psychology of each tribe. It is the accepted policy of the Indian government that in the process of "developing" the tribals there should be no interference with their basic way of life and that any changes induced should be gradual and as far as possible in conformity with their own traditions. According to Prime Minister Nehru, "We should not over-administer these areas or overwhelm them with a multiplicity of schemes. We would rather work through, and not in rivalry to, their own social and cultural institutions."[2]

Of the several tribal areas in the country, NEFA has been the most isolated. There is no non-tribal population within NEFA apart from government officials. The jungles are so thick and the roads so few that to penetrate the interior still requires a major expedition, while until recent times the economy of the people was confined to barter exchanges and bead money. In British times there was no regular administration in this region. It has been organized only since independence, and now for the first time the people of NEFA are beginning to have schools, hospitals, roads, and other such elementary civic amenities.

[1] Boys' dormitory.
[2] In a foreword to the second edition of Verrier Elwin's *A Philosophy For NEFA.*

I

In a Gallong Village

Along, the headquarters of the Siang Frontier Division, is a small
township of bamboo-matting houses with palm-thatch roofs. Lying
in a bowl surrounded by mountains, it overlooks the river Syom,
which later joins the Siang and eventually, at Dibrugarh in Assam,
becomes the mighty Brahmaputra. The town has no road yet to the
outer world, and its population of 1,100—mostly officials and their
families—are dependent upon rations and other supplies air-lifted
from Dibrugarh.

The village of Kombong is a six-mile ride from Along over a
narrow, winding, but jeepable road made entirely by the villagers.
The mountain slopes are thickly covered with vegetation,[1] and there
is smoke in the air because the people are clearing the forest—*jhuming*
as it is called—for the next sowing. On the slopes here they practise
dry paddy cultivation. They do not plough, but simply break the
surface of the earth and dibble in the seed. They cultivate each patch
for two years and then leave the land fallow and let the jungle grow
over it. The forests are demarcated on village basis and the village
council allocates land for cultivation to each family, according to its
needs and labour capacity. There is no permanent individual ownership of land. Ploughing and permanent wet paddy cultivation is now
being introduced in the valleys for the first time.

In this region of Siang, there are two main groups of tribes, the
Gallongs and the Minyongs, both belonging to a larger group known
as Abors or Adis. The Minyongs are more close-knit communities,
the village being the basic unit of organization. The Gallongs are
more sophisticated and display a greater clan than village solidarity.

Kombong is a big village with 158 houses, all built on wooden
platforms raised on piles high above the ground and each at some
distance from the other. The house consists of one large, more or
less square, room with two fires, round which the family eats, drinks
and sleeps. Outside is a narrow platform which is used when the
weather is sunny. For a latrine, despite the jungle all around, each
house has a little closet and open ground below, and plenty of pigs.
The moment anything drops the pigs clear it. Though an outsider
may take a little time to get used to the accompanying grunts and
scramble, it is a highly practical solution of a problem that has proved
very difficult in the rest of India. For there are no human scavengers

[1] Average rainfall in NEFA is 200 inches per annum.

in this society. Pigs are the scavengers, and since they are not human there exist no taboos against them.

Gallong women wear a white *lungi* type of skirt called *galle* reaching below the knees, and a short-sleeve blouse. Jewellery is mainly of beads. The men are dressed in a loose coat-like upper garment and a *langty* with an apron in front. Legs are bare, with muscles well developed from all the walking and climbing they must do. Each man wears his knife in its bamboo casing. The *gams*, or official village leaders, wear red coats. Facial features are mongoloid and the skin colour pale.

Revolt of the Young

We sit around a fire. The room is pitch dark. Only the fire lights up the faces. The rice beer, *apong*, goes the rounds in "glasses" made from fresh-cut bamboo stems, and rice and meats are served on banana leaves.

The men recall, not without nostalgia, that the British used to give them many presents—rum, tobacco and salt, and many other things, but mainly rum. A major improvement since independence, however, is that while previously "we could not enter the presence of an official unless we wore trousers", now the officials mix with them freely. Also they are now getting drinking water, schools, and above all roads, though they still do not have any road beyond Along and, as Binsen Lollen says, they are keen to get out and see the country.

"Of course, the greatest difference in the last decade is the security we enjoy now", continues Kibi Ado, another *gam*. "Ten years ago a man did not dare go out of the village after dark. Even to the fields and the forest we would go only in groups, for fear of being kidnapped and sold into slavery. Now we have no such fear, and we move around freely."

Kibi smokes several *bidis*, recalling the old times. Then the conversation turns to the attitude of the younger generation, for it is they, naturally, who have felt the greatest impact of school education and of the new contacts and influences to which NEFA has been exposed in recent years. In keeping with the official policy of gradual change, there are no spectacular projects of development in this region. Besides building roads, schools and hospitals and providing for drinking water facilities, the major emphasis in NEFA is to encourage indigenous arts and crafts, such as weaving and wood carving. In agriculture the plough is being introduced for the first time in valleys suitable for wet-rice cultivation. But education, even though it is especially orientated to the tribal background, does introduce entirely new concepts and values.

The elders recall how, even 20 years ago, young men never refused to work or to obey their elders and the *niyam* or custom of the village. "The only time they might resist would be if they had forcibly captured a *mithun*[1] from a neighbouring village and we would ask them to return it because it would involve the whole village in a retaliatory raid." They would resent that and prefer to fight. "But otherwise they used to be very obedient and hardworking. If anyone was not, his body was simply cut up and thrown into the river. But now they know that no one will punish them really severely any more. 'What can you do?' they say. They are not afraid of anyone, either in their own family or in the *Kebang*."[2]

"What about the girls?"

The elders are even more vehement about them. "They are worse than the boys. They marry whom they like now—even water-carriers.[3] And they leave their husbands", wails Kibi in a tone of despair and shock, "if they do not like them."[4]

The Main Difference

In Roying village in Pasighat sub-division,[5] Adul Ering, an elderly *gam* who wears a felt hat, blue beads and a white loin cloth, has a son in college. Adul holds that the impact of education is not bad. Some boys, even though educated, continue to be obedient. Others who do not go to school may be disobedient. "But this I will say: when we were young we used to work extremely hard. Our boys still work, but not as hard."

To this Abong Tabing gives the reply. He is young, perhaps twenty years old, handsome, almost pretty, with a dimple in his chin. He wears a felt hat, a green coat over a white vest, navy blue shorts, boots and socks, and a watch.

"We have seen the difference between the old and the new times", he says with a serious mien. "The main difference is not that we do

[1] A species of wild buffalo, highly prized among them.
[2] The village council.
[3] He means government servants.
[4] In this tribe matches are arranged by parents, and often a grown girl will be married to a baby boy. So there are plenty of unequal marriages.
[5] Pasighat is a bigger town than Along though it is only a sub-divisional headquarters in the same Siang Frontier Division. There is no electricity yet in Pasighat, but it has a high school—the only one in NEFA so far.

not work hard but that we try to use our brains more than our fathers did. Our fathers just went into the forest and did *jhuming*—shifting around here and there. We now do permanent cultivation and we produce more. If I get money I would not purchase beads with it but would use it for opening a shop and doing business. I have seen the Marwaris[1] and others making a lot of money in that manner. If we open shops we can compete with them and make money."

"No", he says, "I do not want to leave the village and live in a town or city. But we want to develop more land for permanent cultivation, as well as roads and business."

The people here are Minyongs. Their houses are made on some-what lower piles than those of the Gallongs, but there are the same pig latrines. There are no village slums or segregation of living quarters on caste basis, and there is little overt difference between rich and poor and no social stratification on that basis.[2]

Minyong girls are uninhibited, and sex life is natural and free. Premarital relationships are common and permitted in this tribe, though a high standard of marital fidelity is enforced. As Yamong Jerang, an intelligent young woman in the village of Ledum expressed it: "We prefer our system of marriage to yours. How can life be happy if we have married a man without even seeing him?"

The Squirrel's Head

Minyongs, of course, are only one of the many tribes, and in many respects they are immeasurably more advanced than most of the other tribes in NEFA. They are, for instance, casteless, almost class-less, exceptionally co-operative, now peaceful and law-abiding and extremely honest.[3] According to the teachers, boys in school do not require any supervisors during examinations. "They will not cheat or copy even if the book is in front of them."

Tosing Ering, a Minyong teacher at Balek, says: "If a man steals or tells lies more than once or twice among us he is considered to be diseased. The normal, according to our values, is the truthful." The

---

[1] Members of a trading and business community coming originally from Marwar in Rajasthan, who have spread widely throughout India.

[2] The main classification in Adi tribes used to be between slaves and free men. Even after the slave had been freed, intermarriage was not permitted. The slave and the master would, however, sit round the same fire and eat, drink and dance together. There is no slavery now among the Minyongs.

[3] It is interesting to note that according to anthropologists these qualities tend to disappear as soon as a tribe comes in contact with a so-called "higher" culture and the process of de-tribalization or acculturation sets in.

villagers' precious possessions and paddy are kept in granaries which are well out of the village—at times one or two furlongs away—so as to escape destruction in case of fire. These granaries are never locked, and thefts are exceptionally rare.

Their village institutions, such as the *Kebang*, or tribal council, and the *Bongo*, in which a number of villages are represented by their leading *gams*, are truly effective. Once a decision is taken by them there is no question of disobedience. During the discussion—often it will go on for several days together—two parties may fight like dogs. But once an issue is settled there will be no subsequent rifts or dissensions.

In villages where there is plenty of land it belongs to the *Kebang*, and every family is free to take as much as it wants and can cultivate. Only in the valleys, where land is limited and permanent cultivation is being introduced, is individual land ownership now being encouraged by the administration.

Minyongs are extremely hard-working and self-reliant—men and women, rich and poor. It does not occur to them to look down upon manual work as menial. They fence in the entire cultivated area of the whole village—even though it might be several miles in circumference. A house or dormitory is built in one day, because everyone helps. Moreover, they are often highly and intelligently responsive to new techniques and methods and alert to economic opportunities. They are taking avidly to wet-rice cultivation, and no sooner has the plough been introduced, than the demand comes for the bulldozer and the tractor. They have heard only vaguely of these giant machines which can work wonders, but they want to use them to clear the forests.

Though they are an extremely isolated and primitive people their egalitarianism and social attitudes are truly impressive. In fact, the impact that many of the tribesmen make on the non-tribal members of the NEFA administration is in several respects even more interesting than the impact of the administration and its development programmes on members of the tribes.

Officials serving in NEFA are drawn from all parts of India and they have to live and work in conditions of isolation, inconvenience and danger which can be but dimly conceived by the outsider. Yet even the humble village school teacher, for example, who has generally a poor reputation throughout India, plays a remarkable role in NEFA. He looks after social welfare, agriculture, medical

work, road making—everything and anything that may come up—
even though he is not paid for it and is not officially ordered to do
so. Very often he is the only official in the place and the only literate
person, so that all government instructions to the village *gams* are
routed through him.

I asked these teachers how it happens that in NEFA they have
apparently not only reconciled themselves to the difficult and primitive conditions, but have succeeded in imparting to their work an
interest and spirit of service which most of their counterparts in their
respective home States seem conspicuously to lack.

The unanimous reply is that the explanation lies in some quality
of the local communities. They mould the teachers to their way of
life. "Their affection and respect is so overwhelming that now we
feel uneasy and uncomfortable when we go back home among our
own people", admits a young Sikh from distant Punjab. "The villagers here of course never enquire of us of what caste we are, which
is normally the first question in our own village way back home",
another teacher from Kerala explains.

"And yet most of these teachers are 'rejected' people, who have
not been able to find jobs in their own States or nearer home",
according to a senior official in NEFA. "They come here originally
for the sake of the job only."

What applies to teachers applies to officials of other departments
as well, be they overseers, doctors, clerks or administrators. In
NEFA most of them seem to acquire a broader outlook, a more
democratic attitude and in fact almost a new personality, whatever
the cadre in which they serve, even to the extent of forgetting their
caste and religious taboos. Often they adopt the local foods and way
of life, and vegetarians and *Brahmins* become meat eaters. A Political
Officer told me he was once astonished to find a vegetarian *Brahmin*
school teacher not only sharing his food with a tribesman but trying
to split with him the head of a squirrel![1]

Medical Versus Tribal Charms

From Khela, headquarters of Tirap Frontier Division, to Margherita there is a motorable road through mountain scenery that is
often breathtaking. In places the forest is so thick that even a rabbit
would find it difficult going. No wonder wild elephants here begin
to use the roads as soon as they are constructed.

[1] Rats and squirrels are relished by these tribes.

At Ledo, near Margherita, begins the famous Burma Road, built during World War II and extending through Burma into China all the way to Kunming, 1,079 miles away. Pangsu Pass is on this road, atop a hump on the Patkoi range which divides India from Burma. Five miles on the Indian side from Pangsu Pass is Nompong, a small outpost. Here is a school with a hostel. The land and buildings—the structures are of bamboo matting—have been donated and built by the villagers without any contribution from the government.

We talk late into the night by the flickering light of a hurricane lantern—the Base Superintendent at Nompong, the school Head-master, an Assistant Civil Surgeon and an Assistant Political Officer, all representatives of the administration and of the civilization and culture of the plains in the heart of the jungle and tribal land.

They are in a reminiscent mood. Only ten years ago the school master had to approach parents with presents to persuade them to send their children to school. "Now I have to refuse admissions." In 1955, when 70 men from Waka came to Dilli base camp and saw a railway train for the first time, they described it as houses walking. And once, after a Political Officer's wife visited a school in her "New Delhi make-up", all the red ink was missing the next day; it was on the girls' lips. On a road under construction near Nainu, Wanchoos refused to cut a certain portion of it unless two black dogs were sacrificed and their heads put on stakes at the site. In parts of Tirap there is a taboo on cultivating land which has been struck by lightning.

It is the doctor, of course, who has to contend most with tribal superstition and to compete with the local medicine man and priest. People here attribute disease to hostile spirits, or ghosts of the dead, or to the breach of some taboo, and therefore expect that its cure also must lie in spiritual measures known only to the tribal priest and the medicine man.

"I have often to tempt children with sugar cubes and their elders with *bidis* and by drinking their beer with them", the doctor says with a smile. In a conspiratorial whisper he adds: "My wife still does not know that I 'drink'." She has remained behind in his home town where their children are going to school. "But what to do— this is the only way I can win their confidence."

The doctor has to tour his entire area on foot. He may have to walk as much as 12 to 14 miles in a day over this mountainous terrain.

"When there is a birth, you know, no outsider can even enter the village and no one from outside the family circle can go inside the house. But now, sometimes, if the case is difficult, they call me in. Normally I let them observe their own rites as well—of sacrificing a chicken and reading the omens from its liver and so on, so that they may feel happy and reassured. Yes, they are very, very superstitious. They have different kinds of charms to drive away the various spirits of disease. The slightest——"

"Tell me, Doctor, what are you wearing on your arm?"

"Oh, this," he stammers and fumbles under the short sleeve of his white shirt, where, tied to black threads, are three small copper containers. "These . . . oh these . . . they are charms."

A qualified doctor of modern medicine, he is wearing three amulets on his right arm and two more round his waist, he informs me. "They are meant to provide protection against danger and to counteract unfavourable planetary influences of Mars, Saturn, and so on. My wife insists that I wear them."

ASSAM AND ORISSA

CHAPTER XVIII

AGRICULTURE WITH DIGNITY

ACCORDING to social scientists, one of the distinguishing character-
istics of a tribal society is that its beliefs and attitudes display narrow
regional and group peculiarities reflecting, perhaps, its extreme isolation and absence of education, mobility and intellectual communication with larger societies.

Even in comparatively less isolated and technically non-tribal communities, however, at an admittedly higher plane of culture and
intellectualization, many incongruous and eminently irrational beliefs
and attitudes persist with an astonishing resilience, also on a narrow
regional or group basis.

In the Kathiatoli Block in Nowgong district of Assam, for example,
the population is non-tribal. It is by no means isolated and it has the
further benefit of having been covered since 1953 by the Community
Development programme, the underlying purpose of which is precisely to induce change in the rural areas by introducing new ideas
and modern techniques. What is more, many peasants here are
Muslim and therefore, theoretically at least, immune to caste taboos
of various kinds which afflict Hindu communities. Thus in the
Rangaloo primary *panchayat* consisting of three villages, only 26
families out of 342 are Hindu. Some 37 of the Muslim households
and all the Hindus are native Assamese, while the remaining Muslims
(279 families) are immigrants from Mymensingh, originally in Bengal
and now in East Pakistan. The immigrants, however, are of long
standing, having settled here 30 to 40 years ago.

These Assamese Muslims and Hindus and the immigrant Mymensingh Muslims have thus been living together for several decades,
often in the same village under identical conditions.[1] Yet, not only
are these immigrants reported to be better cultivators all round and
more hard working than the native Assamese—even the cow of the

[1] Like the Bagdis and the Sikh *Jats* in Shri Ganganagar district in Rajasthan.

Mymensingh peasant yields more milk than that of the local farmer—
but the pattern of their cropping here, and, I am told, throughout
Assam, continues to differ basically.

Rangaloo is a single-crop paddy-growing area, where work is required in the fields for less than three months in the year. Cultivating
vegetables in addition to paddy is highly remunerative; they all admit
it. Yet only the Mymensingh Muslims cultivate vegetables on a commercial scale, exclusively or in addition to paddy. Their immediate
neighbours, the Assamese Muslims and Hindus, grow mainly paddy,
with only a few vegetables exclusively for domestic consumption.

In the hamlet of Sengmora, for example, there are 25 families of
Mymensingh Muslims cultivating 901 *bighas*[1] of land and 25 families
of Assamese Muslims owning 944 *bighas*. While the immigrants have
80 *bighas* under vegetable cultivation, the Assamese peasants have
only 20 *bighas* under vegetables. Within the same Development
Block there is the wholly Assamese Hindu village of Pachim Kawai-
mari Kotohapara, where the 50 families cultivate 689 *bighas* of land,
of which only ten *bighas* are under vegetables.

Mymensingh Muslims were, it appears, the first to introduce
vegetable (and jute) cultivation[2] in Assam, but what is surprising is

---

[1] Three *bighas* = one acre.

[2] In most parts of India, in fact, and among Muslims also there are only certain
castes and communities who cultivate vegetables on a commercial scale; the general
class of peasants does not. There is an interesting observation on this subject by the
poet Rabindranath Tagore, though he refers to the situation in his own State of
Bengal. Writing in the *Modern Review* of December, 1925, in an article entitled
"Striving for Swaraj", he says: "I have close acquaintance with the farmers of at
least two districts of our province and I know from experience how rigorous for
them are the bonds of habit. One of these districts mainly produces rice and there
the cultivators have to toil hard to grow their single rice crop. Nevertheless, in their
spare time they could have raised green vegetables around their homesteads. I tried
to encourage them to do so, but failed; those men who willingly sweated over paddy
would make no effort to grow vegetables. In the other district the cultivators are
busy all the year round with rice, jute, sugar cane, mustard and other spring crops.
But certain holdings which are not fit for such produces are left fallow, a wasting
asset which must bear the landlord's rent. To this same locality come peasants
from up-country who lease the fallow pieces of land, raising on the sandy soil several
varieties of melon, and they go back home with substantial profits. The producer
of jute can by no means be called lazy. I am told there are other places in the world
quite as suitable for growing jute, but the farmers shrink from the hardships of its
cultivation. If Bengal has a monopoly of jute, it is due as much to the character of
its peasants as to its soil. And yet these hard-working jute cultivators, with the
example before them of the profits made year on year by the up-country melon
growers, would not follow it up on their sandy soil, since it would mean treading a
path to which they are unused.

"Faced with such a problem, the difficulty we have to contend with is to draw the
people's mind from its old path of habit into a new one. I cannot believe that it will
do any good to indicate an easy external method; the solution hinges on a change of
mentality."

that they continue to hold a virtual monopoly of it. Since a good number of them are concentrated in this Nowgong district, the district is famous for its vegetables. They supply vegetables as far as Dibrugarh on one side and Shillong on the other, usually at inordinately high prices. But the local population refuses to follow suit and share in the profits. And it is not because they are unaware of it; the example is at their doorstep.

There is Omar Ali, originally from Mymensingh. He has no land of his own, but takes some on lease. He grows only vegetables and purchases his paddy. There is black-bearded Hazarat Ali, also originally from Mymensingh, who also cultivates vegetables and some jute and mustard. Famood Ali, however, an Assamese, owns 16 *bighas*, but his entire land is under paddy, one crop only. Not that he is even reasonably well off. Except for the few big landowners in the village, none of the peasants of local origin have any surplus paddy to sell—for their own consumption even it does not suffice for the year. Landless families[1] take land on a crop-sharing basis and must pay, they claim, 50 per cent of the produce to the landlord by way of rent, although according to the law[2] they should pay one-fifth only. But the non-immigrants among them will not increase their income by growing vegetables commercially, because, as Famood Ali expresses it:

"For one thing, we have no experience—it depends on habit. Mymensingh people have it; we do not. Secondly, it requires more labour. Thirdly,[3] the Mymensingh farmer will grow his vegetables and take them to the market in a basket on his head or on *bhar*.[4] That we cannot do. It is below our dignity. If we do not take it ourselves we will have to hire a servant to do so; that would be expensive and the servant may cheat."[5]

---

[1] In the three villages of Rangaloo Primary *Panchayat*, 107 families out of 342 are landless.

[2] The "Adhiar Protection and Regulation Act", 1948.

[3] This is really the crucial and decisive factor.

[4] A bamboo slung across the shoulder with a basket suspended at either end.

[5] The same problem does not arise in the case of grain because, firstly, the small peasant has none to sell, and, secondly, buyers generally come to the fields to purchase the grain and it is their responsibility to remove it. It is this same sense of "dignity" which generally prevents an Assamese from working in tea gardens or from driving a bullock cart, or in fact from doing any kind of manual or earth work, such as making roads, or even building the plinth of his own house, the superstructure of which is entirely of bamboo and thatch. Almost all such work in Assam is done by imported labour from such distant States as Bihar, Orissa and Andhra. Yet more than 1·2 million Assamese are estimated to be landless in the plains districts of Assam, while 52·3 per cent of its agricultural population holds less

What is dignified for the Mymensingh Muslim peasants in Assam, such as carrying of vegetable loads to the market, is not dignified for the native Assamese, although they live in the same villages, some of them at least profess the same religion, and they all practise the same profession, agriculture. Either they are tenants or they own roughly the same amount of land and enjoy the same social status that goes with property.

A Story of Three Villages

Similarly, in the eastern State of Orissa there has been completed recently one of the biggest power, flood control and irrigation projects of modern India at Hirakud. It has an installed capacity to produce 123,000 kw. of power, while its 16-mile dam across the river Mahanadi, claimed to be the longest in the world, is designed to irrigate in the first stage about 672,000 acres.

Just as in the Tungabhadra region in Mysore, in parts of Orissa also there is a general resistance to using the irrigation waters, although paddy is the main crop. The prevailing belief here is that one cannot grow paddy or any other crop twice on the same land in the same year, though this is exactly what the Hirakud waters now make feasible. To induce the change in the cropping pattern, the State government is not only giving irrigation water free for the time being but it is constructing the field channels as well, which are normally the peasants' responsibility. Within the compact area of a single district of Sambalpur, where the Hirakud project is situated the following variations in the peasants' attitude to the project were encountered.

In the village of Budelpali the local agricultural extension officer had to go on hunger strike—he lay down in the village temple and refused to take any food—before he could persuade the peasantry to sow for a second irrigated winter crop of paddy. He had already brought 250 *maunds* of seed and distributed it to them. The peasants, however, had put forward the familiar excuses that: "Paddy cannot grow a second time on the same soil; our *kharif* production will fall; the water is without its electricity;[1] where will our cattle graze?" But

[1] Often villagers believe that if power is made from water, the water loses its electricity and therefore some valuable property. Hirakud is a power and irrigation project.

than ten *bighas* of land. In West Bengal, also, many communities among the peasants consider it below their dignity to take their farm produce to the market for sale. This must dominate their entire attitude to surplus production.

they would not readily agree even to try an experiment which promised straightaway to double their income.

In Pradhanatikara, on the other hand, another village in the same block of Baragarh less than ten miles away, the peasants were most enthusiastic. They required no persuasion whatever and raised no difficulties. "Actually", says one of them, Sugri Pradhan, "we did not believe that we would ever get these waters. We first heard of the Hirakud project nearly 15 years ago. We could not believe that the Mahanadi could ever be dammed and its waters brought here, and, if man could do it, we felt he must be God. No. None of us went to work on the dam."

Another, Ashta, continues excitedly: "The day we saw the water coming it was early in the morning. We were leaving for the *hat*. But when we saw the water in the canal we turned back."

"It was a Friday[1]—1st of *Asadh*",[2] interrupts Doitari, an old man with a hooked nose. "The sun was just rising when we saw the water. That week we did not even go to the market, we were so happy."

"To me the water looked like milk", again cuts in Sugri. "In fact, we believed it to be Ganga *jal*.[3] So we came home and then went back to the canal with offerings of rice, coconut and flowers and we worshipped it. . . ."

Within the same district there is a third village, Champaparda, right at the Hirakud project site where the dyke ends on the reservoir side. It is the only village in the area which escaped inundation. Yes, they had all had land but it has been submerged. Because their sixteen cottages were not inundated, however, they decided to take cash compensation for the agricultural land and continue to live here.[4]

"The produce from the land we had was enough to meet our needs for about three to four months in the year. For the rest, we had to supplement our income by making *bidis*", explains Etwah. Nowadays, however, *bidi*-making is the only work they do, and the income from it barely keeps them alive. When the earthen dyke was under construction they worked on it for nearly four years, although, according to Mangra: "We do not know why the dam was built."

[1] On every Friday there is a weekly market, or *hat* as it is known locally, at Baragarh.

[2] June–July.

[3] Ganges water and therefore holy.

[4] The rest of the people of the area have been shifted to new sites where land was available. These villagers also could have chosen to shift. They would not have had to go very far, since there is a large area of virgin forest land in the district.

They worked on the dyke only for four out of eleven years, because
after that time they would have had to go to work at some distance
from their homes, since the work nearby had been completed.[1] What
is even more incredible, they have not yet seen the main dam.
Champaparda is about eight miles from the main dam, on its left
earthen dyke. The peasants of Champaparda have gone up to the
eighth mile of this dyke which they helped to build, but not beyond.
Not a single man from this village has gone to see the main masonry
dam or the power house. "We have heard that there is a house from
which electricity comes out. We haven't gone to see it because we are
not interested."

And yet, of the three peasant communities,[2] they alone came into
direct contact with the entirely new and modern techniques, urban
men and gigantic machines which were imported into the heart of
this jungle to build the project. Two new townships have grown up
near it since. The peasants of Champaparda alone actually witnessed
and participated in the construction of the dam. In fact, it would be
difficult to conceive of a more radical and rapid transformation of an
environment which had been absolutely primitive. Yet the people of
this village have been the least affected by it and have evinced
practically no interest in it.

Darkness at Night

It is around 10:30 at night at Champaparda. The huts have very
low walls and thatch. Outside of one of them, two small, naked children
lie asleep on a piece of cloth spread on the ground. By the roadside
which runs near the village a couple of men, shirtless, are furiously
busy cutting into shape *kendu* leaves,[3] while a woman is equally
absorbed in rolling the *bidis* and tying them with thread. More such
groups are busy in the same manner across the road. To their immediate right is the reservoir, a 288 square mile stretch of deep dark
waters. The stars are not reflected in it and there is no moon.

The light the men and women are working by comes from the street

---

[1] The project was started in 1948 and took eleven years to complete. At the time
of peak construction, during the last three years, more than 30,000 labourers were
employed. Most of them were imported from other States.

[2] Of the three communities, only the residents of Champaparda are tribal—
Araons. But unlike the tribesmen of NEFA they are by no means isolated. There
are non-tribal villages all around them and they are in daily contact with non-tribal
people.

[3] These leaves are used to roll the tobacco in, instead of paper. *Kendu* bushes
grow wild in the jungle.

lamps—mercury blue—a long string of which weaves a beautiful garland of brilliance along the dam and the road over it the whole night through. Beyond, behind the small hill which hides from view the power house and the two project townships, the entire horizon is brightly lit as in the first moments of a brilliant dawn. 500 miles of high voltage transmission lines carry the electricity from Hirakud to distant corners of the State to supply towns, and major industrial undertakings, such as steel, aluminium, ferro-manganese, fertilizer, textile, cement and paper. There is, however, not a flicker of light within the entire village of Champaparda.

"What are we to do with light when we do not have any food in the house", mutters Balku.

When they do have a light it is still the naked, feeble flame of an oil wick.

9. Padam girls in Nefa, husking paddy. (Chapter XVII.)

10. A Minyong girl on the way to collect fire wood. (Chapter XVII.)

11. Gangadhai and Champabati of the village of Champaparda in Orissa, making *bidis*. In the forefront is one of the mercury lamp posts that run along the dyke and dam of Hirakud; by the light of these the villagers work till late at night making the *bidis*. (Chapter XVIII.)

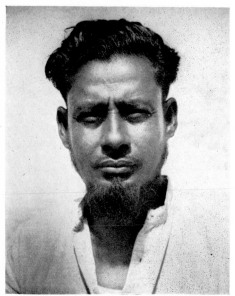

12. Hazarat Ali, a cultivator of Nowgong District, Assam. Originally from Mymensingh, he cultivates only vegetables, jute and mustard. (Chapter XVIII.)

WEST BENGAL

CHAPTER XIX

EDUCATION IN A RURAL SOCIETY

BADAN: "Don't you think, mother, it would be a good thing to give Govin his *háte khadi*?[1] It is a great drawback that I cannot either read or write. . . . . Don't you think it would be a capital thing to teach Govin *lekhá-padá* (writing and reading)?"

Alanga: "Oh, Bábá Badan! don't talk of *lekhá-padá*. Your elder brother was sent to *páthsálá* (school) by your father, contrary to my wishes. And what was the consequence? The gods took him away from us after he had been to school only one year. Reading and writing do not suit poor people like us. I fear the gods will take away Govin also (the son of Shashthi![2] may he live for ever!) if you send him to school." . . .

Badan: "Why, as to death, mother, that is the decree of fate. Whatever is written on the forehead by Vidhátá Purusha[3] must come to pass." . . .

Alanga: "Quite true, Bábá Badan, the forehead is the chief thing. Why, then, should you fight against the forehead? We have been born tillers of the ground, and we must remain tillers of the ground all our life. Besides, did your fathers ever learn to write and to read? Why should you wish your son to do what your forefathers never did?"

Badan: "The days in which our fathers lived were days of piety and virtue. . . . But in our days, men have become very deceitful—they fear neither gods nor men. It is necessary to learn to read and to write, that we may not be cheated and oppressed."

Alanga: "You men can talk a great deal, and bring a great many

[1] Literal meaning: "putting chalk into the hands of a child." It is a religious ceremony performed in Hindu homes at the commencement of a child's education.

[2] Beneficent goddess who takes special care of children.

[3] God.

reasons for what you say. What can a woman say before a man? . . .
If you will have it so Bábá Badan, then send him. May Gopinath
preserve him! But if he is to be sent to school, you must wait a few
days till I spin some more thread, sufficient to make for Govin a
dhuti."[1]

Badan, overjoyed at his mother's consent, readily agreed to the
delay.

The above conversation took place early in the nineteenth century,
when Bengal was under the rule of "Company Bahadur",[2] and it is
recorded in the once widely-read novel, *Bengal Peasant Life*[3] by the
Rev. Lal Behari Day, which gives an authentic account of real people
in the author's village of Shona Palasi, which still survives in the
district of Burdwan. The subject of the conversation is Govinda
Samanta, the hero of the story. Badan was Govinda's father, an
illiterate peasant, and Alanga the child's grandmother.

Bhadra-Lok and Chhoto-Lok

Ultimately, when the *dhuti* was woven for Govinda, he did go to
school for some years, but because of family circumstances he had to
leave school early and go back to become a "tiller of the ground". It
would have been of interest to know, though, what Govinda Samanta
would have done if he had had a few years more of schooling. Would
he have returned to the profession of his forefathers? For it is rare
now to find a boy in the rural areas of Bengal who has been to school
for seven or eight years actually working on the land.[4]

A rudimentary and purely indigenous system of education was not
unknown in Bengal villages even before the British era, though in the
elementary stages it was confined to the teaching of simple arithmetic
and the ability to read and write. The wealthy usually preferred to
engage private tutors. *Pathsalas*, however, such as Govinda attended
were widespread. There were two of them in Govinda's village and
they were self-supporting, for there was no state system of education
then. The teachers were maintained by presents in kind and very low

---

[1] Bengali pronunciation of the word *dhoti*.

[2] East India Company, as it was known then locally.

[3] Macmillan, London, 1884, pp. 58–61.

[4] By and large, apart from a few exceptions, mainly in the mountains, this applies
to the whole country, and it is not because more paying avenues of employment are
immediately available to anyone who goes to school. It is the "educated", in fact,
who face currently the greatest pressure of unemployment throughout India. In
Bengal, for every white-collar job of Rs. 50 per month, there would be at least 5,000
applicants from among the "educated" classes in the rural areas.

fees. Govinda had to pay one anna per month and, in addition, small presents of tobacco, betel nut, and some rations, such as unboiled rice, salt and pulses. Bengal was also the first to receive the benefits of "western education" as it came to be introduced[1] by the British in India in the course of the last century.

Till very recent times, however, education in the villages remained not only predominantly a male monopoly but also confined to the upper castes. In Bengal these were mainly the *Brahmins, Kayasthas* and *Vaidyas*. By general consent the masses were precluded from its benefits, prejudice against their instruction being "nearly as strong and general in their own minds as in the minds of others."[2] Members of the same stratum of upper castes,[3] moreover, were also the big property holders,[4] who still constitute a powerful rural middle class intelligentsia for which Bengal is notable. In this manner, the upper castes, the upper class, and the educated sections all became more or less synonymous, to be known as *bhadra-lok*, meaning the noble or gentle people—a term still very much in current use. The landless masses, who are also the low and scheduled castes and tribes,

---

[1] With the founding of the "Hindu College", or rather school, in Calcutta in 1817. It was the first English seminary to be set up in India. (Rev. Alexander Duff's Evidence, Lord's Second Report, 1853; and Romesh Dutt, *Economic History of India in The Victorian Age*, Kegan Paul, London, 6th ed., p. 199). This, however, was "private enterprise". The British Parliament ordered for the first time in 1813 that a sum of £10,000 be appropriated for the education of the people of India in the three Provinces of Bengal, Madras and Bombay. But nothing was done about it for another ten years, till 1823, and only in 1832 did the Bengal government appoint a Committee of Public Instruction.

[2] From Adam: "Reports", Long, 1868, p. 254—quoted in *The Cambridge History of India*, Vol, VI, p. 102.

[3] With a sprinkling of Muslims and of what may be described as the "middle" castes of artisans, traders and peasants such as *Sadgops, Gorai, Swarnarkar, Teli*.

[4] Thanks mainly to the Permanent Settlement by Lord Cornwallis in 1793. According to an article entitled: "Rural Research in Tagore's Sriniketan", in *Modern Review* of May, 1934:
"When all this mass of data was taken up for analysis and the population classified into economic groups it was found that such grouping on a purely economic basis corresponded remarkably closely with the social groupings according to caste and religion. . . . We do not have to ask a man's occupation; we have only to know his caste or his religion and we know his economic position." Even the cattle have different evaluations: "the high castes have the highest priced cows, the Santals' cattle are barely animals that manage to stand on their legs. There is difference even in the average price of chickens and ducks kept by one class and another." The survey pertains to nearly 450 households in a cluster of four villages near Sriniketan, in Birbhum District of West Bengal, in 1933. Re-surveyed in 1956-57 by the same team, the situation was found to be basically unaltered. Of course, 70 per cent of the Santals and 90 per cent of the low castes are landless and "have no share in the ownership of the only means of production available in the villages." Hashim Amir Ali, *Then and Now*, Indian Statistical Institute, Calcutta, 1960, pp. 33–34 and p. 54.

and illiterate, are aptly referred to as the *chhoto-lok*, or the small people. Apart from caste and property qualifications, the most distinctive feature of the *bhadra-lok* is that they do not work with their hands. The *chhoto-lok* are the "labouring" or the "serving" classes.

CHAPTER XX

"HE IS NOT MY FATHER"

IN the course of the last decade, the spread of literacy in West Bengal has been phenomenal,[1] though, the balance is still heavily with the *bhadra-lok*.[2] While this imbalance may be only temporary, what may not be so temporary is that the concept of education has acquired in *toto* the attributes and attitudes of the *bhadra-lok*, a social meaning and status which bears no relation to its content. Whoever gets educated today, irrespective of his social and cultural traditions and the economic circumstances of his family and community, acquires invariably the upper class prejudices and postures as well, the most outstanding of which, as already stated, is a strict aversion to and disdain for manual work. He leaves agriculture altogether, because cultivation, or in fact any kind of manual work in the rural context, is considered totally incompatible with education. The result is that the spread of literacy among the peasant classes helps to improve neither the techniques of cultivation nor agricultural production—the two most pressing problems today in the agrarian field. Instead of being utilized to improve agriculture, education is looked upon as an avenue of escape from it.

[1] Thus, whereas in 1947–48 the total number of students in West Bengal (in all institutions) was 1,682,064, in 1956–57 it was 3,475,480, according to the West Bengal Directorate of Public Instruction. The State authorities have decided to make primary education free and compulsory throughout the State during the Third Plan period (1961–1966). Total population of West Bengal (1951 census) was 26,302,386 in an area of 34,214 square miles.

[2] According to the 1951 Census, roughly 70 per cent of the *bhadra-lok* would be literate as against eight per cent of the *chhoto-lok*, although literacy for all "agricultural classes" (members of society, who depend primarily on the agrarian economy) in West Bengal was computed at only 13 per cent. The "middle castes" would boast of about 16 per cent literates. And yet out of a total population of these "agricultural classes" of 13,939,105, the *bhadra-lok* would number only 103,881 and the *chhoto-lok* 5,920,449. (In the census classification *bhadra-lok* would correspond to the "Non-cultivating owners of land, agricultural rent receivers and their dependents", and the *chhoto-lok* to the "Cultivators of land wholly or mainly *unowned* and their dependents", together with "Cultivating labourers and their dependents".)

As a school teacher in Birbhum district put it: "Only education makes men of us.[1] But education and cultivation cannot be combined. The two must be kept separate. How can a boy who has been to school do the hard labour which cultivation requires?"

This conviction is universally held, though for varying reasons. There is in some instances the usual inherited caste prejudice which we have come across on several occasions elsewhere, and education has been unable to destroy the dogma underlying it. Thus another village school teacher, Bannerjee, admits, "Yes, of course, I could earn much more if I cultivated the land myself. But since I am a Brahmin, I cannot do it. I will not plough." He has ten acres of land, cultivated entirely by employed labour.[2]

"Why will you not plough—from conviction or simply because you are afraid of society? You are an educated man and you are expected to teach your students the importance and dignity of manual work. How do you reconcile your education with this outdated and irrational prejudice? Would you plough yourself if you went away to some distant place where nobody knows who you are?", I ask Bannerjee.

Even after thinking it over he persists: "No, I still would not touch the plough. I do not allow my sons to do so either. But then I am only a primary school teacher. There are *Brahmin* teachers in high schools and colleges and they also will not plough, although they are much more educated than me. Yes, I do believe that a *Brahmin* should not plough and that the tradition should be maintained."

Sastiram is another landowning school master. According to him: "We too could get much more income if we worked ourselves. I am not a *Brahmin*; I am a *Kayastha*. But I cannot work because we have a certain status in society to maintain. My father did not work on the land, so I also do not do it. Though with us it is not strictly a religious ban, it would be beneath us to work on the land ourselves."

Sadgops, like the *Aguris*, to which caste Badan belonged, however, are professionally an agriculturist caste in Bengal.[3] They are excellent cultivators and have no inherited prejudice against handling the

---

[1] There is a popular saying in Bengali that a *chasa* (agriculturist) can never imbibe culture.

[2] They never give up the land, even if they do not themselves cultivate it. Ownership of land gives status; to work on it is derogatory.

[3] There are such communities in every State, known by different names. They are professionally agriculturist by caste. They are generally good cultivators, whatever their circumstances, and they work themselves.

plough or doing manual work. But even among them, those who get
some education now wholly abandon their inherited way of life.
There is Fakir Mandal, an elderly man. He is a *Sadgop*, and his is
the biggest and wealthiest family in the village, having the largest
holding of land, 200 *bighas*.[1]

"I am not a *babu*"[2], says Fakir with obvious contempt. "I am a
real farmer. My hands will prove it." He stretches out his rough and
gnarled hands proudly. "See my *dhuti*—the coarse cloth I wear. I
have worked myself all my life with my own two hands." This, despite the large property he owns and the social status he must enjoy
by virtue of it.

Yet Fakir's sons and grandsons are all *babus*, simply because they
went to school. Not one of them is working with him in the field.
It is beneath them now. Kanai, a young boy of about eight, one of
the grandchildren, dressed in shorts and a nylon bush coat, takes off
in our presence on a bicycle. Fakir shrugs his shoulders. "What can
I do? These are the changes of time. How can I stop it? If the *babu
chasas*[3] go to the field even, they must go on a bicycle. How can they
be expected to work? How can they ever become good and efficient
farmers? They require fine clothes, sun glasses, watches, bicycles,
fountain pens. The whole environment has changed. Even if I have
to sell my land I must provide them with these. But they do not
work." And in the case of his family at least there can be no plea that
it has no land, or that the holding is too small to meet the new
aspirations for a higher standard of life.

As with *Sadgops*, so it is with other communities, even in instances
where caste is not a prejudicing factor. In Sansat a group of Muslims,
representing the landowning educated middle-class of the village,
also refer to themselves as "*ami bhadra-lok*".[4] Though they are all
agriculturists they do not work themselves but use hired labour entirely. Abdul Rab, a young man and a school teacher from among
them states frankly that: "A boy who has been to school up to the
seventh or eighth class and who in the company of his friends sees
his father working in the field will tell his friends that 'he is not my
father'. He feels so ashamed of him."

Besides this attitude to work, the new values inculcated by education seem to appertain almost exclusively to consumption. As they

---

[1] Three *bighas* = one acre.
[2] White collar worker.
[3] Gentlemen cultivators.
[4] We the *bhadra-lok*.

said in Sansat where all the *bhadra-lok* young are educated or in school, "In the last ten years no new *pucca* houses have been built in our village; nor is there any improvement in our tools of cultivation. But yes, the number of cycles has increased, and torches, watches, goggles and fountain pens. Transport costs have gone up. We would walk seven miles to Bholpur when we were young. Now the young people must go by bus and spend five annas per trip. Dress also has become more expensive. But because of it all consumption of necessities has gone down. Where else or how else could it be adjusted? We are definitely eating less, and our diet is much poorer than what it used to be.[1] We now take less milk, meat, fish and eggs."

Like Fakir Mandal, Sumed Ali, a big, well-built man with a small beard, complains: "If my son wants a bicycle I must provide him with one even if I have to sell my land. I must give him because otherwise he will get angry. We have to cut down on necessities to provide the young men with all these things."

The impact of education is similar even among the Santals, who are a tribal[2] people and constitute the main body of agricultural labour in West Bengal. They are on an even lower rung than the *Harijans*, and outside the Hindu caste hierarchy; their entire life and tradition is nothing but hard manual work of every kind. Both their men and women work in the fields.

However, in the Santal village of Kapastikiri several boys go to school, though none has passed out of it yet. Schooling came here for the first time two years ago, by way of a primary school, but in the neighbourhood is an older high school, in which there are thirty Santal students now. Every one of the school-going boys present says he would prefer to take a white collar job rather than be an agriculturist like his parents.

Among them is Dhirendra Nath, smart, short and slight, in blue

---

[1] This increase in the consumption of durable consumer goods like bicycles and torch lights, and deterioration in respect of food, drink, etc., appears to be widespread and has been noted in many surveys undertaken recently in various States. Thus, according to a socio-economic study of Sahajpur, a village in West Bengal: "It is significant that the effect on the consumption level of the villages has already been judged adverse by the villagers. The opinion survey showed that the majority of the people, even among the better-off sections, like cultivators of land wholly owned, thought that their consumption level in respect of most items has deteriorated since 1951." J. P. Bhattacharjee and Associates, *Sahajpur*, Visva-Bharati University, Santiniketan, 1958, p. 142.

[2] Unlike the tribes of NEFA, the Santals are not isolated but come in daily contact with the non-tribal communities around them, from whom they tend to imbibe many values that are different or even contrary to their own. They get more "Hinduised", so to speak.

shorts and no shirt. His father has five acres of land, a large property for a Santal. He is a big man in the village. Dhirendra Nath, however, says that: "After I have finished my studies I will serve in an office and give my land to share-cropping. Well, for one thing, cultivation is so difficult. It requires hard work. Secondly, I can also help the poor by letting them have a share in my land. I will earn enough for myself by doing another, more pleasant job."

"Yes", he asserts without any hesitation, and the rest agree with him, "in my opinion manual work is meant for the poor and the illiterate. Those who get educated should do better jobs." He is still in school, but because he has become literate he already feels superior to the class to which his father belongs.

The *chhoto-lok*, therefore, when they do send their children to school nowadays, tend to withdraw them early. As Girish Karamachari, the village blacksmith in Sahajpur, said: "It is not possible for us to allow our children to become *babus*. Unless we work we starve." No boy in his family has been permitted to pursue education, if at all, beyond the fourth class, and every one of them still works in the family smithy, which is in a shed outside the cottage.

The Young Versus the Old

Another interesting result of the spread of education in rural Bengal is that an acute division appears to have taken place between the generations—the more educated younger people versus their largely less-educated or illiterate elders. At times and places the resultant tensions are extraordinarily bitter, which is a somewhat unusual phenomenon in India where the tradition is for the young to respect age almost unquestioningly.

Since in the rural areas education of more than primary standard is still confined largely to the children of the *bhadra-lok*, this split between young and old exists mainly within the ranks of the same class. When a young man from the *chhoto-lok* does go to school for a sufficient number of years, not only does he acquire almost invariably the attitudes and values of the *bhadra-lok* but he endeavours also to "cross the line" and join the younger group of that class, even if it be only on the periphery. In every village, in fact, the younger educated elements form a separate exclusive group, and there is generally little communication of ideas or values between them and the rest of the population.

At the time of my visit, the first elections to the newly instituted village *panchayats*[1] are taking place. Up till now only "Union Boards" have functioned in the rural areas in Bengal, and the franchise was confined to tax-payers. The Boards have been abolished, and now the vote has been extended to all adults, who will elect a village *panchayat*, which will constitute the primary unit for rural development and local self-government.

Although generally the election situation may be described as unpatterned, since alignments are neither clear nor uniform, being based mostly on village personalities and factions, the antagonism and rivalry between the young and the old is to an impressive extent in open evidence.

There is an awareness that "these elections would create a conflict between the labour class and the *bhadra-lok*" who employ labour. "Labour is now trying to organize against us, to crush us", say the elders among the *bhadra-lok*. But, actually, this organization is nowhere in evidence, and the vocal partisans for and against the class of *chhoto-lok* are drawn almost entirely from the ranks of the *bhadra-lok* themselves.

There is Bishen Pal, a candidate—stout, unshaven chin, spectacles. He was educated in Calcutta and is now a village school master. But he says that he represents the poor, and that is his main qualification. Usually, it is the younger elements that claim to be the true champions of the depressed classes.

There is Abul Halim, with a bearded face and dressed in *dhoti* and *kurta*. He is very young, and you can see the fire in his eyes. A teacher in a high school, he is also a candidate for election. He owns 60 *bighas* of land. But he wants to fight his own class, whom he describes as "the exploiters and reactionary elements of society—the older people and the ex-*zemindars*".

There is another very young teacher who wanted to join the contest but was found to be under age. His name is Rabindranath and he is a graduate. His complaint—and he is very bitter—is that younger people are unable to get any foothold in society. "Young blood is being ignored and is not respected. That is our complaint. We think the older people are reactionaries. These elections have divided the whole village—father from son and even husband from wife." He is very angry because, according to him, "some scheduled caste people wanted to contest the election here, and we are convinced that their nomination papers were deliberately rejected because if they got

---

[1] Instituted under the "West Bengal Panchayat Act" 1956.

elected they would unite against the reactionary forces". Two other young teachers in the same neighbourhood agree with what he says and they express the same views and sentiments. But they themselves are all unquestionably from the ranks of the upper class and castes.

Revolution in Shona Palasi

There is one village where the change in leadership on the basis of age has actually taken place. Its name is Shona Palasi, about which Rev. Day wrote in his *Bengal Peasant Life*. In outward appearance there is perhaps little difference in the hamlet from the days of Alanga and Badan. The approach road is still as bad, and even a jeep cannot negotiate it if there is a slight shower, when it becomes a slippery field of treacherous mire. The old tanks, temples and at least the ruins of many of the houses and monuments mentioned in the novel are still there. But the leadership in this village now is all young.

In the previous Union Board, I am told, "the members were all middle-aged or old. The president was forty-five years old. They were all from the landowning class and of upper castes." The first change came when an experimental village *panchayat* was established here and elections were held for it in 1956 on an adult franchise basis. Eight young school teachers residing in this village[1] decided to contest these elections as a group and they won. "Now the village affairs are entirely in our hands. The older people are left only with social and religious affairs. The *panchayat* is totally ours."

The *panchayat* has 13 members, and between the two villages of Devagram and Shona Palasi, which jointly constitute a single *panchayat*, the age group of its members is now 25 to 30 years. Only one member is 35. Jeevan Biswas, the president, is 29 years old.

The struggle for this leadership started, according to Jeevan Biswas and his colleagues, in 1950. "We organized a society of young people called *Sakti Sangh*." Jeevan was its president. It had about 25 members. "The idea came from school life. Most of us were together in school, and boys going to college were then living in the village. We all went to the same high school two miles away. We also got ideas from the cinema and our contacts with people in Burdwan.[2] We go there frequently—at least once a week—and meet many outsiders."

---

[1] In all, the village has 33 per cent literates, of whom ten persons have received college education.

[2] Burdwan, nine miles away, is a large town and district headquarters, 66 miles north-west of Calcutta.

By 1955, however, the *Sakti Sangh* was destroyed because, according to them, the old people did not like it. "They felt we were against them. They were very angry with us and they tried their best to harm us." Finally, the old people went to the extent "of involving us falsely in a criminal case, and that finished the *Sangh*. What happened was that a man committed suicide by hanging himself inside our club room, which at the time had no doors or windows. We were accused of murdering him and were arrested. The case went on for seven months. We were all acquitted. But the records of the *Sangh* were taken away by the police and the room was sealed." Nine members of the *Sangh* were accused, including Biswas. The *Sangh* was thereby totally destroyed. But the group alignment survived.

"Older people were afraid that we would tutor the poor and that they would refuse to submit to their exploitation", is the explanation given for this unnatural and highly unfriendly action on the part of their own elders. "Older people who are still strongly opposed to us are small in number now. They are dying out. They should die. It will be better if they go. They are of no use to us. The whole nature of society will change as soon as they go. All problems will be over", says one of them, a school teacher, 23 years old. "As soon as these old people go, we will get our chance to be free and mix with the *Harijans* and others freely and more liberally. At present we are unable to do it openly because our old guardians are very conservative", declares another.

Jeevan adds: "The one big difference between us and our elders is our attitude towards the poor. We feel for the poor. Our elders are still in the dark, interested only in village factions and politics. They do not even want to make the people literate because they fear the working classes will get out of control. We, on the contrary, are very keen to educate them."

And yet not a single landless or scheduled caste peasant is a member of this *panchayat*, despite the undoubtedly sincere sympathy and compassion its youthful members feel for that class. One *Harijan* was elected in 1956, but his election was declared invalid because, it seems, he was not on the voters' list.[1] Biswas and his friends, who form the core of this youthful group in power, are all from the educated upper castes, the same *Brahmins*, *Kayasthas* and *Vaidyas*.[2]

[1] No *Harijan* was elected in the 1959 election either.
[2] Generally, this phenomenon of *panchayats* being dominated by the upper castes would be the same throughout India. Therefore, special provision is usually made for the nomination of a *Harijan*, if he is not elected.

Inevitably, Shona Palasi has inherited the same traditional pattern of education, the distribution of property and the power that goes with it, that prevails in most West Bengal villages. True, the village *zemindar* is no more.[1] Nevertheless, whereas 90 per cent of the upper caste families in this village own land averaging 15 *bighas* per family, only 20 of the 131 low-caste households have any land. Their average holding per household works out at 0.93 *bigha*. Further, out of a total of 285 households that make up Shona Palasi, 91 families holding 68 per cent of the total village lands do not cultivate the land themselves because they are prevented by tradition and social custom from doing so.[2]

The pattern repeats itself in the field of education.[3] On the whole, the village population boasts of 33 per cent literacy—which is high. But whereas among the upper castes 59 per cent are literate (67 per cent males and 51 per cent females), among the *chhoto-lok* only five per cent can read and write. This may be taken, of course, mainly to represent the legacy of past neglect and indifference, though Shona Palasi has never been without a school since the days at least of Govinda Samanta—that is, for at least a century and a quarter. In fact, whereas in Govinda's time there were two *pathsalas* in the village now there is just one, and it is still only a primary school with four classes. But it is financed and run by the District School Board. Not only is the school entirely free, and has been so since 1948, but primary education in this village is also compulsory.

Nevertheless, after eleven years of free and now compulsory education, only 40 per cent of all the boys and 35 per cent of the girls in the age group of six to eleven years actually attend school, and that, too, fairly irregularly. The corresponding figures for the *chhoto-lok* are still five and four per cent respectively.

Against this formidable backdrop of acute imbalances in the village community, the programme of its present youthful *panchayat* consists of "road development, making of culverts, and improvement of sanitation, drainage, library, village security and recreational activities".

[1] All permanently settled *zemindaris* were abolished and taken over by the State in 1955, under the "West Bengal Estates Acquisition Act", 1953.

[2] Another 21 per cent of the land is held by non-cultivating castes for whom cultivation is not a traditional occupation but a source of side income, so that only ten per cent of the land is held by a class which treats agriculture as its true profession and works at it accordingly.

[3] Statistics for Shona Palasi have been collected personally by the author and checked and supplemented from the yet unpublished work of Tara Krishna Bose entitled: *The Bengal Peasant—From Time to Time*.

Biswas explains further that they are very keen to run a social centre for adult education to make the *chhoto-lok* literate, but are unable to do so in the absence of a grant from the government. They require about 20 rupees per month.[1]

"But why?"

"Oh, for oil for light and a teacher."

"Surely oil won't require more than a monthly contribution of four annas from each of you, and you are all yourselves trained school teachers. Only a village without any literates must pay for a teacher. Even if each of you took a turn once a week and gave only one hour in the evening, it would be sufficient."

"You have put a very difficult question", is the reply. "But you know we are poor people. No teacher will be prepared to spare the time without remuneration."

Moreover, although the young leaders feel strongly for the poor they themselves continue to display all the attributes of the *bhadra-lok*. Not one of them is working on the land himself. "Even if we wanted to, we are physically unfit now and also mentally untrained for agricultural work. Our heredity does not permit hard labour", they say frankly.

The widowed mother of Biswas, Bhibabati, intervenes to confirm with some vehemence that "my son does not even know how to put a bullock in the cow-shed, or to mix its feed, or to split a bamboo for the thatch. He knows nothing about *zemindari*[2] affairs. I have had to manage everything ever since my husband died 18 years ago." On the other hand she complains of her son's extravagance. "He never wears a *dhuti* costing less than 8 rupees. And every day he requires at least 32 cups of tea for his young friends."

Obviously, therefore, whereas the young and educated leaders of Shona Palasi are no gain to the agricultural economy of the village, since it can have no benefit of their new knowledge and enlightenment, the "revolution" in its leadership also is one of age only, and not of class or caste relationships. And though in theory the situation could be pregnant with exciting possibilities, actually it has made no significant difference to the fundamentals of the situation, social or economic. There has been no shift in centres of power or influence.

---

[1] They were getting a grant from the local Community Development Block previously to run an adult literacy centre, but it was stopped, it seems, because the centre was not working satisfactorily.

[2] Here *zemindari* means: simply pertaining to the affairs of the land and agriculture.

Perhaps it is too early to judge. Perhaps it lies beyond their power to change. It would surely be naïve to expect a voluntary surrender by those in power of their privileged position, especially in the absence of sufficient pressures from below.

The poor and the scheduled castes, in fact, seem barely aware of the split among the *bhadra-lok* over their cause. They have not even united to take advantage of it. In the village of Bahiri, the voting is being held on the particular morning that I am there. There are eight candidates for four seats. Groups of men, shirtless, squat on the ground outside the Union Board Office, awaiting their turn to cast their votes. They are the *chhoto-lok*. Not only is no one from among them a candidate, but they are neither excited nor agitated, not even animated. They have come to vote, but say they do not know why or what for. Many have not heard the name of the extinct Union Board, and one or two who have, do not know what it was. They seem to know even less about the newly instituted *panchayat* they are now electing. The whole attitude is one of apathy and total unconcern.

MAHARASHTRA AND HIMACHAL PRADESH

CHAPTER XXI

MACHWAS AND APPLES

PROPHETS of change repose an immense faith in education as its most dynamic and infallible instrument. The mere fact of change thus induced may not, however, suffice. For its extent may not be adequate, nor, at least in the first instance, its nature and direction desirable. It may be irrelevant or even adverse in relation to the exigencies of a particular situation.

In Bengal, for instance, or for that matter anywhere else in India, because of the social attitudes associated with education, there is no indication that the spread of education among the peasants will help in the foreseeable future to increase agricultural productivity. Education does not even improve the economic mobility of the individual. It opens up new avenues but closes off others. For example, it rules out working on the land altogether. The new limitations are just as severe and often additional to those already imposed by caste and social status. They are self-imposed but nonetheless effective. What is more, the situation is not peculiar to agriculture. It is similar in other fields as well, such as fishing and mining.

The village of Karla on the west coast of what is now the State of Maharashtra, in the district of Ratnagiri, is inhabited entirely by a Muslim fishing community known as Daldis. Only a generation ago this village had in operation a sizable fleet of big (five tons and more) deep sea fishing boats of local design called *machwas*. They could sail 40 to 50 miles out into the open sea and catch even big fish like sharks; what is more, they could operate throughout the year. As 85-year-old Mohammed from this village, who spent 40 years at sea, recalls: "My father was a fisherman, and his father before him, ever since we know of. We worked as *khalasi*[1] on other people's boats

[1] Hired hands on a profit sharing basis. The actual catch is shared between the proprietor and the *khalasis*. The latter are like the agricultural share-croppers.

13. A group of women of the Choudary tribe, to which Gainabehen and her family originally belong, in Surat district in Gujerat. (Chapter XXIII.)

14. Another woman of the Choudary tribe in her typical dress and jewellery. (Chapter XXIII.)

15. Portrait of a patriot—Gainabehen. (Chapter XXIII.)

16. "Bapu's Kuti"—the hut in Sewagram *ashram* where Mahatma Gandhi lived from 1936 onwards. (Chapter XXIII.)

17. "All is silence, empty." Bapu's room inside the hut in Sewagram *ashram*. (Chapter XXIII.)

and used to go on the *machwa*. As soon as we would return home we would leave again—not wait even for a cup of tea. . . . Oh yes, I have seen many storms. In spring especially storms come very unexpectedly. . . . In my time there were 50 *machwas* here and seven or eight at a time would set out to sea."

Now, in this same village, the number of *machwas* has dwindled to two. Only the small *hodi* and *tony* types of boats are in use.[1] They go out with the tide and return with it and they fish in coastal waters only, always in sight of harbour lights and only in fair weather. They never risk a storm and cannot venture out during the four months of the monsoon.

This fall-off in deep-sea fishing naturally means much lower catches. According to Mohammed: "Our catch of eight days at any time between November and March used to be more than they get now in a whole season." As Ahmed and his companion *khalasis* of another village confirmed that night when we were out at sea in the little five-oared boat: "Our life is very difficult. We are unable to provide two full meals in a day. We cannot afford to purchase the ration, so we buy a small bun for one meal and eat only one—just plain." He holds up one in the moonlight to show it to me. "It costs one anna, you know—one anna!"

But they will not go out for deep-sea fishing, not because of any shrinkage in the market or fall in prices. Both have improved beyond measure with the development of roads and modern transport facilities into the hinterland. There were no trucks in the time of Mohammed. Runners used to carry the fish in baskets on their heads to the off-coast towns, while for curing they used to have to use the salty sand from the beach. Now, they have a proper salting yard provided by the government, which also provides the salt.

But the present generation of fishermen will not go out to sea because, in their own words: "Our forefathers were ignorant and illiterate and so did not mind the hazards of fishing in *machwas*. It meant staying out at sea for ten to 15 days at a time. It also meant fishing all the year round. With enlightenment and education, young men now prefer to go in for service[2] rather than work on *machwas*. It is therefore difficult to get the men" (even among illiterates like Ahmed) "to man a *machwa* now. So the number of these boats has

---

[1] They have outrigger equipment for balancing and safety.

[2] "Service" is throughout used in the sense of any salaried job. It may be with the government or a private firm.

L

fallen off. All young people coming out of schools are looking for other jobs and giving up fishing. Only those who are no good at studies stick to the trade."

Hazards, inconvenience and hard work are thus considered incompatible with education and enlightenment. Consequently, even Mohammed's own sons have not taken to the family occupation. He further explains sadly: "You see, in my time service was looked down on and we took pride in being independent fishermen.[1] We did it not just to fill our bellies but also because we had a genuine love for fishing. But now it is the other way round. Fishing is considered to be a low profession and service carries prestige. Besides, our work is of toil and sweat. There are no short cuts here. You can earn only through honest hard work. No, I did not go to school, but our young people who do, go away to Bombay and get easier jobs."

Those serving on the small boats also are all illiterate, hired men, usually on a catch-sharing basis. The owner of the boat does not go out on the boat any more either, though he did in Mohammed's time. He is "educated" now.[2]

Similarly, a coal miner's son today who goes to school would never dream of going back to mine coal like his father and his father before him. Anandi Sahu and his colleagues, all miners for generations in a colliery in Dhanbad district in Bihar, some of whom are now sending

---

[1] Although he was only a *khalasi* and never owned a boat himself.

[2] In Ratnagiri is another interesting example of two communities living side by side for generations but not learning from each other. Here the Muslim fishermen of the Daldi community, for example, are far more prosperous than the local Hindu fishermen, because for one thing, Daldis have bigger boats and superior equipment by way of nets, hooks and line than the Hindus. The Hindus' boats are only one-man *tonies*, they fish mainly in the creek and use only hook and line with small hooks. Secondly, the Daldis also trade in fish, retail and wholesale. Thirdly, the Daldis alone salt the fish. The Hindu fishermen on the other hand, do not salt or cure the fish, with the result that whatever they catch they must sell fresh, the same day. What they are unable to sell in the local market by sundown, they dispose of at any price, or just throw the fish in the gutter. But they will not salt it because it is not the custom or tradition with them to do so. Daldis, in fact, buy wholesale from the Hindu fishermen at low prices, and then salt the fish and sell it far into the hinterland at a handsome profit. Yet the Hindu and Muslim villages are side by side.

The difference in incomes between the Daldis and Hindus is reflected clearly in the appearance of their villages. Mikriwada, a Daldi village, for example, has many *pucca* houses, tiled roofs, furniture inside. Their women are well-dressed and wear a certain amount of gold jewellery. The children also are properly clothed and most of them are attending school.

In the village of Mirya, on the other hand, where all fishermen are Hindus of Bhandari community, the huts are small, with mud walls and thatched roofs. The people are poorly dressed, and the children are naked, under-fed, and thin and pale. The whole atmosphere is one of depression and severe poverty.

their children to school for the first time, ridiculed the suggestion out of hand. "What an idea", they said. "It is like the saying we have: '*padho pharsee becho tel*'—that a man should study Persian[1] and then sell oil. How can that be?"

In Kotgarh

In one instance where I came across a transformation in the economy and way of life of a people, the primary cause (if any single factor can ever bring about a socio-economic revolution of any substance) was not education—but apples. Education has followed the apples. It did not precede them.

The total area is approximately four by five miles, with a population of less than 10,000. High in the mountain in the State of Himachal Pradesh, it is called Kotgarh, in Mahasu district. Half the area is still under forest, and the rest is partly under apple orchards.[2] It produces 70,000 to 80,000 *maunds* of fruit per annum—of a gross value of Rs. 3,000,000, according to 1958 figures. The famous Hindustan–Tibet road goes by Kotgarh. It was opened to vehicular traffic only 15 years ago. Earlier, it was a mule track, and apples had to be exported also on mule-back. Now trucks rush them down to the rail head at Kalka.

Bare mountains all around; there is a skyline here of snow covered peaks and a very narrow valley in the distance with a glimmering streak. It is the river Sutlej on which the Bhakra dam has been built a little further down. Here are lovely shady walks, through forest and orchards, old and new, wild rose creepers in bloom—all white, shifting purple shadows. On the apple trees the fruit is still small and green, with touches of deep red like rouge: budding temptresses. Families that only three to four generations ago were carrying loads of stone on their backs are rich now—truly rich, thanks entirely to these apples.

The story of a typical family, picked at random, will better portray the extent of change in this area—the story of Saranpat.

"When I was eight years old, my mother sent me to the free

---

[1] Implying scholarship. In Moghal times Persian was the court language—hence the prestige.

[2] In the whole of Himachal Pradesh State only 3,000 acres are under fruit, mainly in Kotgarh and some in Kotkhai. The Government is now trying to extend the area to 10,000 acres. Ninety-four per cent of this State's population is dependent on agriculture.

Mission School here. On the very first day the master said I must have the Urdu primer. It cost one anna. When I asked my father for one anna, he gave me such a thrashing with a stick that I have never forgotten it. He told me to go and graze the cattle instead. 'I have no money to give you', he said. I told the master and he gave me an old used primer which was all torn and thumbed. But in any case, I could not continue beyond the fifth class. . . .

"Father used to cultivate wheat and maize. But the cereal barely sufficed to feed the family the year through. He was always in debt and had to work as a coolie besides. Labour was paid six *pice* to two annas daily, and there was plenty of *begar*—carrying of loads for the government and its officials at that time. My father did a lot of *begar*.

"Our old house was of the conventional type. It had three rooms on the ground floor. The cattle were kept in them. The family lived on the second floor; steps to it were by *sigah*, a single log in which steps were cut. In one room upstairs there would be an *angithi* in the centre, and everyone slept around it. One room was used as store room and in one, the smallest one, would be the kitchen. The rooms had no windows and the doors were only four and a half feet high, while the walls were made of stone packed with wooden planks and the roof was slate."

Today, though Saranpat's wife's dress has many patches and he says he has not yet purchased even an ounce of gold,[1] he has a magnificent six-room double-storied house which he started building in 1956, and he will not rest till he has added another floor to it. In every room there are built-in cupboards and windows. The roof is of tin, as is the fashion here, and not of slate. There is a kitchen and a broad verandah in front, godowns below and a separate shed for animals. The house has wooden floors and ceilings and all the woodwork is polished. He has three sons, all educated. The wife, fair complexioned, tall and slim, is dressed in a long brown woollen gown called *rejata*. A cotton printed scarf is tied round her head.

This change in their fortunes is due predominantly to one factor: about 15 years ago the family took to planting an apple orchard. "Now the trees are full grown and I make 50 times more than my parents", says Saranpat proudly. He has only 15 *bighas* of land, but it has already promoted him to a standard of life undreamt of by his parents. What is more important and significant, he and his family

---

[1] People here generally do not spend money on clothes and jewellery. They prefer to invest in property.

continue to work as hard and conscientiously as their forebears, despite the higher income and education which the younger generation has since acquired. Only the wife is still illiterate; she says her husband has not taught her because "he himself knows so little". They employ no permanent labour in the orchard; only in the picking season they have to get some help to get everything done on time.

Since Grandfather's Time

In Saranpat's grandfather's time the mainstay of the family was 500 sheep and goats, though there was plenty of land and the population was much smaller. In those days peasants did shifting cultivation here, as in NEFA.

"When the first land settlement was made here in the 1880's, I think, the people were so poor that they gave up their land rather than pay the land revenue", recalls Saranpat. "For clothing in those days a man would possess just one woollen coat tied with a waist band. He did not wear shorts or even a pyjama underneath. Every family did its own spinning and weaving of woollen materials. They did not burn oil for light, but pine bark. Utensils were made of mud and wood, and the food was very simple. Only if one fell sick did he drink *kadha*—tea with honey and other spices. Sugar of course was unknown. Now everyone drinks tea."

Not only is everyone in the neighbourhood drinking tea these days, but also every one of the old houses has been or is in the process of being torn down and replaced by a new one, of "new design", with a gleaming tin roof, like Saranpat's. Where less than 30 years ago people of Kotgarh would not accept paper money because they could not make out the difference between "notes" of one denomination and another, today almost all the children, including those of scheduled castes, are in school, according to local sources.[1]

Kotgarh was ceded to the British after the Gurkha war in 1814. While the surrounding territory was left with the then ruling Indian princelings,[2] Kotgarh and the neighbouring Kotkhai were brought

---

[1] According to 1951 census, in the State as a whole less than 8 per cent of the population was literate, while in this particular district literacy was only 3.9 per cent. The present popularity of schools is more recent.

[2] It was only in 1948 that some 30 "Indian States" of the western Himalayas, each till then under its own ruler, were merged to form the State of Himachal Pradesh. Most of them were very small and extremely backward. The smallest, Ratesh, had an area of only two square miles. Himachal Pradesh now has an area of 10,904 square miles and a population of 1,115,536. It is largely mountainous with altitudes ranging from 2,000 to 22,000 feet.

under the Punjab administration, under direct British rule, with the result that missionaries came soon after, in 1843. The church in Kotgarh is reportedly the oldest in the area. To this Mission came a remarkable American, Samuel Evans Stokes.

According to his son, Stokes first came out as a tourist but returned as an evangelist. Later, however, he not only joined the nationalist movement for independence, led an agitation against *begar* and went to jail, but he himself was converted to Hinduism[1] and became Satyanand Stokes. He married a local woman, settled down in Kotgarh, and started an orchard. The Mission already had an apple orchard—it was the first to start it—and there were one or two other orchards belonging to well-to-do people. But Stokes, it seems, not only brought special varieties of this fruit from the U.S.A.,[2] which he tried out himself, but in the 1930's and later he went round with missionary zeal urging people individually to take to apple growing, showing them the technique, and persuading them to give up their traditional cultivation of maize and other cereals, which could barely keep them alive through the year.[3] Above all, he set an example of attitude to work which now pervades the entire population and marks it out as clearly distinct from the adjacent areas and in fact from most areas elsewhere in the country.

According to one of Stokes's sons: "Until only a few years back, we were practically the only family in this whole region which was financially well off.[4] But I still had to work as a coolie in my father's orchard, till the age of 17 I think, and I used to be paid like the other coolies. My children do the same now when they come home on vacation.

"One day, only recently, I was milking the cow when a member of Parliament came to visit us. He was taken aback and said: 'Surely you can afford a servant to do this work. Why do you do it yourself?' I replied: 'It is because I want to go on affording the servant.'"

[1] This gave him an entry into homes of Hindus who otherwise would not even have taken water from a Christian's hands. Moreover his conversion shook the local Hindu society, since its orthodox sections were bitterly opposed to it.

[2] Those varieties are still the most popular. Earlier only European strains were being cultivated, introduced by a German missionary, Rev. Beutel. He was in fact responsible for developing the first Kotgarh Mission Orchard, many years before Stokes came.

[3] The soil here is very poor for cereal crops but excellent for apples. Apples do not require a rich soil.

[4] The father inherited a large fortune and the family's orchards are one of the biggest in Kotgarh. Since the movement to plant orchards started on a mass scale only in the 1940's, the prosperity of Kotgarh people as a whole is very recent.

Stokes's wife, a college-educated Indian girl, also works in the orchard alongside hired women labourers, with a basket tied to her back, just like them.

The outcome is that everyone in Kotgarh claims that he works in the orchard. There is no evidence of any contempt for the work. It is not considered incompatible with enlightenment, education or social and caste status, though, of course, it is a new kind of work, as distinct from routine agricultural operations, and the distinction is probably important. Moreover, local labour has become specialized and in any case no longer performs any work of unskilled nature such as digging, lifting of boxes, etc. For this work immigrants come from Nepal, Hoshiarpur, Kashmir and Chini. On roads and public works, also, all work is done by imported labour. Until only four years or so ago, Kotgarh labour also was doing this kind of work. But not now. It does only technical jobs such as picking, grading, grafting, pruning and spraying.

Furthermore, although superficially there is a polarization in Kotgarh on class basis, the caste base also survives and has in fact crystallized instead of weakening with economic development. Specialization in the various branches of fruit-growing is on caste lines. For example, *Harijans*, as a community, have taken to grafting. Also, with greater economic independence the *Harijans* here are no longer mute nor submissive. They are asserting themselves and have organized, again on caste basis, under the political banner of the Scheduled Castes Federation—all of which appears to increase tensions, both in class and in caste relationships, rather than contribute to inter-caste mobility or greater integration.

Only two decades ago in Kotgarh, if a *Harijan* met a caste Hindu on the road, the *Harijan* would immediately cross over to the *khud* side, and thus concede the right of way to the upper caste man as a mark of respect. Today the same *Harijans* are refusing to play the drum—they being the musicians by tradition for all such occasions as weddings, fairs, and so on. Their boast to caste Hindus is that: "we will make you play the music and be our palanquin bearers". Recently, when one of the *Rajputs* celebrated the marriage of his son and asked for *Harijan* musicians as usual, the musicians refused to go, and he had to do without them.

The Gaddis of Kundi

In other parts of Himachal Pradesh, however, the scheduled castes continue more or less in the same depressed position as of old. Thus, in a village in Sirmur district some *Harijans* recently tried to take a *Harijan* bridegroom in a *palki*, whereas they are permitted only the horse. The result was that they were given a sound beating by the local *Rajputs* for over-stepping their legitimate caste rights.

Elsewhere, not only do the *Harijans* continue to play the drum and sing as usual, but the peasants of other castes also continue to be steeped in deep poverty and backwardness. Here is a scene from Chamba, on the western extreme of the State.

He is small, nondescript, dark, with a stubble on his chin, in shabby tattered clothes full of patches. She, however, is tall and beautiful. He takes a small banjo-like instrument in one hand and with the other beats time with his fingers on a little drum. She plays on small brass cymbals. And then she sings, of the ages gone by, in praise of the Kings and Queens of Chamba,[1] who ruled over them for centuries till a mere decade ago. They are *Harijans*, and she still knows more of that bygone age than of the present, for here there has been no material transformation in their life, outlook, or motivations as in Kotgarh. There are no apple orchards in Kundi.

The village is fifteen miles from Chamba. For most of the way there is a motorable road along the river Ravi, its waters tumbling, swift, noisy, green. The road ends at Chudi, and from there is an almost perpendicular climb on foot of nearly two miles. At Sonara, half way up, the clouds open up and present a breath-taking view of the great and holy mount Kailash. It seems so near, all white in a cloak of snow. And then as the sun sets behind another towering mountain to its left, for a few fleeting, but unforgettable moments the sky is sprayed with gold dust, while the peaks to the right turn a pure burnished copper.

Kundi is on a small plateau. Above and around it is a thick grove of *deodars*, and in its midst a very old temple. The peasants here are mainly *gaddis*. They still sing, with affection, praises of their now deposed kings and queens, despite all that they suffered under them.

In the summer months every year, for example, they used to have to carry, free of any charge, slabs of ice to the palace in Chamba, the then capital, to keep their ruler cool in his palace at a lower altitude in the valley.

---

[1] Chamba, a former princely State, was founded in about A.D. 550 by Marut, a *Rajput*, and was ruled throughout by descendants of the same dynasty till they were deposed in 1948 with the coming of independence.

The snow line in summer here is 10,000 feet above sea level. So the peasants would first have to climb to Bugli Ka Cho, to reach the snows, and then walk all the way down to Chamba—in two stages. Each man would carry one *maund* of ice strapped to his back. If anyone failed for any reason to give his due contribution of labour and ice he would be flogged and thrown into prison.

But the people of Kundi still sing of those days because, though they do not have to do *begar* now, they claim they are worse off economically. In 1955 there was such a deluge here that all the top soil of their miserable patches of earth was washed away. From this flood they have not yet recovered, for a field on a mountain without its top soil can be as barren as the sandy tracts of the Rajasthan desert. Secondly, *gaddis* never live by agriculture alone. They also keep sheep and goats which are useful both for the wool, which they can sell and use to weave their own cloth, and for manuring the fields. Here they use no other fertilizers. The new forest laws, however, have closed the forests for grazing, and the result is that they cannot keep any animals now. Khemtu, for example, used to own 60 sheep. Another peasant, Hodi, used to have 200. Now they do not have a single animal; so not only must they purchase wool, which costs four times the price it used to, but their lands remain un-manured.

In the year 1959 their dress, their houses, their food, and their general poverty, in fact everything in Kundi, appears to be almost exactly as Saranpat said it was in his father's and grandfather's time in the last century. And whereas in Kotgarh nobody now works as a casual unskilled labourer, here in Kundi their main sustenance comes precisely from the daily wages earned by working as coolies, digging and carrying stones on their backs to build roads and public buildings. The peasants cultivate maize and barley or a little wheat, but the yield from their land is so meagre that it does not suffice for even half the year. According to pretty Bajiroo: "We are always hungry."

Their lives, the peasants claim, are no better or different today from what they have always been, except that "once in a while some people come and ask for our votes and promise all kinds of things but never show their faces again".

GUJERAT

CHAPTER XXII

IN KAIRA

OF course, apples do not grow everywhere. In another instance of a rural area—Kaira district in Gujerat State—where in the last two or three decades development has been impressive in the general context, it is difficult to isolate a single such primary agent. It can be ascribed only to a combination of several factors: an inflow of capital earned abroad, native business acumen with the attendant virtues of the predominant peasant community, and the close impact and stimulus of a political movement.

Sixty years ago the villages of Kaira[1] were not very different from villages anywhere else—the same single-storied mud huts and thatched roofs. It has been mostly a *ryotwari* area. At the turn of the century, however, not only was land revenue in Gujerat inordinately high, but in 1900 there occurred a severe famine, so severe that for many years thousands of acres of fertile land lay fallow because there were no peasants to cultivate it. According to Sir Antony Macdonnell, President of the Famine Commission, who visited the district of Kaira in 1903: "The condition of the Peasant Proprietors was wretched beyond description, and the worst of them lived in single rooms with all their family, and with hardly any articles of furniture. The cattle they used was often hired; and any property they had was often mortgaged".[2]

The result was that many families, particularly from the upper and middle class of peasant proprietors, began to migrate from this region to seek fresh opportunities, mainly to east and south Africa. The migrating community were mostly *Patidars*, who constitute the chief

---

[1] With an area of 2,542 square miles, the district has a population of 1,612,426 of which 72 per cent is rural and 28 per cent urban. (*Census of India*, 1951).

[2] Quoted in *The Economic History of India in the Victorian Age*, by Romesh Dutt, Kegan Paul, London, 6th ed., p. 492.

farming and landowning section in this region. They are known for high mobility, a shrewd eye for business opportunity, excellent husbandry in agriculture, and above all a consuming ambition, combined with the necessary will and drive to make money. The last has an interesting motivation, though of course it may not be the only one. It seems, the dowry a *Patidar* father must pay to marry his daughter is extremely high. Not only must he earn the necessary cash for the purpose, but he must own a decent house in his village and have some agricultural land with a well to give him the requisite status. But while the dowry system exists elsewhere in India and generally contributes substantially to the peasant's burden of debt, among the *Patidars* apparently it is responsible for their greater wealth and an unusual degree of success in whatever trade or calling they may follow—including agriculture.[1]

A typical example of individual enterprise among the *Patidars* is Mathurabhai Ramdas of the village of Boriavi. A short, thin man with hands gnarled and knotted, hair grey but teeth intact, he is now about 70 years old. His father owned 20 *bighas*[2] of land and a small mud hut, its one room partitioned into two. "In one half the cattle used to be tied and we lived in the other half." They had one well worked by two bullocks. Their food never consisted of anything superior to bread made of *bajra* or *kodri*.[3] "Our cooking was done in earthen pots."

Neither Mathurabhai nor any of his three older brothers went to school. "I started working in the field at the age of 14 or 15. Before that I used to take cattle out for grazing, fetch grass and water, and do other miscellaneous jobs."

From his father he inherited five *bighas* of land about 40 years ago, and worked it jointly with another five *bighas* of one of his brothers. Today that same property has increased to 70 *bighas* without any extraneous assistance or capital beyond the earnings from the land itself. Besides, Mathurabhai now owns a tractor; on the farm he has an imposing three-storied brick building with electricity, and two more houses in the village. He also has two wells, both fitted with electric pumps, so that his entire land is irrigated. He has paid 10,000 rupees in dowry for the marriage of each of his two daughters.

---

[1] Originally they were all agriculturists. Their caste also is that of professional agriculturists.

[2] One acre = one and three-quarters bigha in this area.

[3] A very inferior quality grain.

His explanation: "I believe in work. It was my ambition to be a good cultivator, and I have established a reputation for good farming".

Which indeed he has, not only because of hard work—he still works himself even at his age and despite his wealth—but because, even with his limitations of total illiteracy and lack of any initial capital stock or resources, he had sufficient ambition avidly to seek out and acquire every possible new technique and tool available to improve his output. In his time, there was no National Extension Service to bring the knowledge and facilities to his doorstep, or to coax him to utilize them. Even a Persian wheel as an irrigation device was a novelty.

A glimpse of two or three predominantly *Patidar* villages, picked at random in Kaira district, will further illustrate perhaps the ambition and energy of this community's approach to life.

There is Sunar village with a population of 5,000, of whom 80 per cent are *Patidars*. The total area under cultivation is only 800 acres, so that the *per capita* holding comes to a quarter of an acre. Only two or three families have ten to twelve acres of land—which is the biggest holding. Yet all *Patidar* houses are made of brick or concrete and are mostly double-storied. The village has electricity, and every house has a water-tap connection because the village built its own water-works nearly 20 years ago at a cost of about Rs.150,000.[1] Sunar runs its own kindergarten school, the building of which cost Rs.10,000. There is another primary school in a handsome double-storied structure costing nearly Rs.40,000, also privately financed. For boys only, it accommodates 400 students. There is a separate primary school for 300 girls, its building worth about the same amount. Then there is a co-ed high school with 600 students; one man from the village has just donated Rs.200,000 for its improvement and extension. Forty boys from Sunar are studying at the University.

There is a dispensary and a maternity centre in the village, run by the Local Board but housed in buildings provided by the village—one costing Rs.20,000 and the other some Rs.60,000. Besides, there are separate libraries for men and women. The village has a clock tower—a familiar landmark throughout Kaira—and a guest house, and now they are planning a town hall. Apart from these and the conventional double-storied residential houses, there are many modern single-storied cottages with garden compounds, such as are found generally in Bombay suburbs.

[1] Almost every village here has its own waterworks.

At the time of the famine in 1900, Sunar had only mud walls to show. Its present affluence comes not from earnings from the land alone, of course, but results from the fact that so many of Sunar's people emigrated to more profitable areas and occupations. Members of at least 300 families went to Africa, mostly to engage in trade and business. Even now six families are in Calcutta, exporting tea to the Middle East. Twelve are in Aden, engaged in tobacco sales. Twenty-five families are in the business of retail distribution of tobacco, and they have their own shops in different parts of India, tobacco being the main cash crop of Kaira. But all profits come back to the village because of that quarter acre of land these emigrant families continue to hold. Ownership of some land and a house in the village is a matter of status with a *Patidar*, no matter how wealthy he may become.

It is the same story in Karamsad village, many of whose families also went to Africa. This village is the home of one of India's most distinguished national leaders, the late Sardar Vallabhbhai Patel— first a close lieutenant of Mahatma Gandhi and later a very important minister in the first national government.

When Sardar[1] was young, he and his brothers went to a primary school in an old shed. His father, a simple farmer, had only three acres of land (which the family lost to its tenants in 1957 thanks to the latest act of land reform). Their ancestral home was of mud walls, "as in fact most of the rest in the village were", recalls Kashi-bhai, the 79-year-old, sole surviving brother of Sardar Patel. Not only are all the houses now in brick or concrete, but "there have been tremendous social changes in my time in every respect. For example, *purdah* is practically gone." Karamsad now has a high school with 1,000 pupils, while 160 of its students are attending college this year, of whom 50 are girls.

Kavitha on the other hand, another predominantly *Patidar* village, is especially impressive in the pattern and extent of its development because it is founded entirely on local initiative and resources. In Kavitha there is only one family returned from Africa, and it receives no money from outside sources. The total population is 3,320. The average holding per family is two acres; the maximum ten. Cash crops are bananas and tobacco. Yet, like Sunar it has pre-primary, primary and a high school—the latter with a magnificent science wing—a public dispensary, maternity home, library and clock tower. Here again, every house has electricity and running water. Within

[1] Vallabhbhai Patel was generally known simply as Sardar, a title meaning chief.

the village there are two cars, five trucks, three tractors, six tobacco-processing factories, and one *bidi*-making factory. The tractors and trucks are also available on hire and are busy all the time. "In the last year alone, the residents of this village have purchased machinery worth Rs.100,000", says Chotobhai, one of the farmers. "We are our own technicians and engineers."

Moreover, out of the 1,448 acres of land cultivated in Kavitha, over 1,000 acres are irrigated. The 400 acres still dry are so because they are situated at a distance, with another village intervening. The village has 50 wells and 18 irrigation pumps, all owned by the peasants themselves, individually or jointly, and the extra water—Rs.300,000 worth per annum—is sold to neighbouring landowners at a fixed rate. Distribution channels for this water—cement pipes—are laid underground. But not a rupee was taken from the government to build this elaborate system of irrigation. In fact, the villagers say that they do not like to take money from the government, nor do they borrow from money-lenders. "We help each other—without any documents even. The secret of our success is that, firstly, no one here is doing only one thing and, secondly, we co-operate with each other." These people do not believe in having just "institutions" either. "They are created primarily to deal with the government. Our *panchayat* does only municipal work", says Ranchodbhai with a snigger, the *panchayat* being a government-created institution. "Formerly *Harijans* used to do the sanitation work. Now the *panchayat* does it."

This attitude of self-reliance and general indifference, if not actual contempt, for official assistance and institutions is widespread among the *Patidars*, and is notable because it is exceptional. Elsewhere village communities are often torn into factions, and individuals spend thousands of rupees just to get elected to the presidency or even just membership of the *panchayat*.[1] In the village of Gopalpura here, on the other hand, it is difficult to find men willing to accept the honour. Its residents waste no money or time on elections. "We select one man from each street. What is there to fight about? There is no wealth to be divided", says Shonabhai. In fact no one is keen to become the *Sarpanch* because: "We simply order him around: 'Come here; clean this street; do this; do that.' Also it is his painful duty to welcome all visitors."

---

[1] In some villages in Andhra it is known to run into five figures, and even murders are not unknown during elections.

"Yes", admits Narayanbhai, the *Sarpanch*, "everyone orders me around." They have literally had to compel Narayanbhai to be *Sarpanch*. "And now they won't even relieve me", he complains.

In villages elsewhere, frequently nothing seems to get done unless the government takes the initiative and gives financial assistance as well for building of roads, schools, and so on. In Kaira, however, in many instances the government could not possibly afford to give subsidies in the form of "matching" grants. In one village, for example, the residents spent Rs.200,000 on a primary school building and then good-humouredly asked the government to contribute the equivalent under the NES scheme, which of course it could not possibly do.[1]

Secret of Success

The sharp business acumen, resourcefulness and energy of this *Patidar* peasantry of Kaira is undeniable and the main cause of its extraordinary affluence and success. These qualities were further canalized by the nationalist movement for independence which swept the country in the first half of the century. This movement seems to have provided the inspiration, the new norms and values, and the necessary purposeful direction for the corporate effort which made this degree of rural development possible. For though the political revolution was unquestionably an all-India phenomenon, and there were outstanding leaders in other parts of the country, Gandhi, himself a Gujerati, chose to concentrate in Gujerat, to make of it an example and to try out in it first the political, economic and social experiments which he personally directed. The result was that, the particular areas he chose, such as Kaira, Ahmedabad and Surat (where also there are many South African-returned *Patidar* families) had the benefit of a much more intimate impact of his personality, as well as that of Sardar Patel, than other parts of India.

Here it is necessary to recall that the Indian National Congress under Gandhi never isolated the political aspect from the social and economic problems. Gandhi insisted that the latter were as important as the struggle for freedom, and must be tackled simultaneously in an integrated manner. He therefore devised an elaborate plan of

---

[1] Under the NES scheme, in the construction of a new primary school building, the villagers are expected to contribute at least 40 per cent of the cost and the rest may be paid by the government. It varies. But this provision envisages school buildings on a very modest scale. Normally, a primary school building under the NES scheme would never cost more than 10,000 rupees.

"constructive work" for villages to resuscitate their economy, to make them attractive and habitable for the new and growing intelligentsia of the rural middle class, which would otherwise migrate to towns; and to change the outmoded traditional attitudes and social stratifications, such as those of caste, which inhibit growth.

This plan laid great emphasis on development of village crafts—of which the spinning wheel became the symbol—and other local industries, on co-operatives, on the removal of untouchability, on the abolition of *purdah* and general improvement of women's position in society, and above all on the spread of education. Naturally, in those days, all had to be done entirely by private initiative and resources.

The Charotar[1] area in Kaira, which was the home of Sardar Patel and in the development of which he took a close personal interest throughout, is thus lavishly endowed with educational institutions, almost all of them sponsored and financed by private organizations. Within the 14 miles from Anand to the village of Sujitra there are at least a dozen private high schools. Here also, in the heart of the rural area, on 1,000 *bighas* of what were once village lands, stands a modern residential and teaching university, Sardar Vallabhbhai Vidyapeeth and an Institute of Agriculture, both designed to bring higher education to the villager in his own environment. While the Agricultural Institute was started in 1939, the University was conceived in 1944, and the men who planned it and implemented the plan had neither a rupee in their coffers nor an inch of land to start with. There are nine colleges now in this district, at the University level.

According to Bhailabhai Patel, one of the founders of the University and till recently its Vice-Chancellor, "Earlier in the century there was only one high school in the whole district. The movement to develop schools started in the 1930's and it spread very rapidly." Now at every second or third mile there is a high school and most of them are private, though the impact of education on the younger generation's attitude to manual and agricultural work is the same in Kaira as in Bengal or elsewhere. For the curriculum of studies, both in the schools and in the University here, is the same as that of the rest of India—and so also are the class and caste attitudes. They told me in the village of Gopalpura: "We never send the boy meant for agriculture to school beyond the primary stage. Farming means hard

---

[1] Comprising the four *taluks* of Anand, Borsad, Nadiad and Petlad. Most *Patidars* of Kaira district are concentrated in Charotar and it is here also that Sardar Patel's village Karamsad is located.

work. Those who get educated will not do it. No student of the Vidyapeeth will go back to work in the fields." Peasants' sons who go to the nearby Agricultural School and College at Anand do so only to train for service, not to become better farmers. "Even if a boy becomes a graduate in agriculture, he is useless for work." Among *Patidars* also there are two communities. One is known as *Leva*. Its members do not themselves work in the fields. The other is known as *Kadva* and its members do work. There is no inter-marriage between the *Levas* and the *Kadvas;* the latter are considered inferior.

As already noted, here agriculture is not the sole pursuit of most farmers, though technologically farming is perhaps more advanced in Kaira than in any other district of Gujerat. Most of the agricultural produce is also processed and marketed by the peasants themselves, individually or through co-operatives, which is not generally the practice in villages in most of the other parts of India. Cotton is grown here, but not sold raw from the field. There are co-operative ginning factories, owned by farmers, and marketing of cotton seed is controlled by them as well. Tobacco, the main cash crop, is not only processed, but even the finished product—*bidis*, and snuff, for which it is suitable—is manufactured and marketed by members of the village population and not by outside traders, or middle-men, as they are known. The result is that the profits remain in the village.

Patidars go in heavily for cultivation of cash crops, unlike sub-sistence farmers who play safe with cereals only. Most of the *Patidar* lands are irrigated, again almost entirely from privately owned wells fitted with pumps and, as in Kavitha, with underground distribution channels to reduce losses by seepage or evaporation, as well as to avoid wastage of land which would be required to make the surface channels.[1] Kaira owns the largest number of pump sets, as well as of tractors, of any district in Gujerat.

And though the pressure on land is heavy here—the density of population is 629 per square mile, the highest in Gujerat—every field has a raised boundary which serves to conserve moisture, and on

---

[1] On the other hand, in the sugar growing areas in Bihar where the government has spent some hundreds of thousands of rupees to sink 946 tube-wells to provide irrigation, over 100,000 acres which could be irrigated could not use the water (until 1958) because of non-completion of channels, lack of co-operation amongst cultivators, seepage, disputes about rates, and so on. Many wells designed to irrigate 150 acres I found irrigating barely five acres! In Uttar Pradesh also, wherever I found a government tube-well provided for co-operative use by several peasants, in actual operation it was usually a failure.

M

which grows a cactus hedge to keep out stray cattle. Along the hedge trees are grown to provide wood both for construction purposes and for fuel, so that cowdung is not burnt but saved for making manure. Alongside the hedge a strip of seven to eight feet of land is left free, on which grass is permitted to grow for fodder. This is why Kaira continues to be an excellent dairying area, while in most other regions where grazing grounds have been brought under the plough in recent years there is an acute problem of feeding the cattle and a consequent decline in milk output.

Kaira's most outstanding achievement is the Kaira District Milk Producers' Co-operative Union with 130 feeder village societies and the largest and most modern dairy in India, located at Anand, again entirely a private co-operative enterprise. It supplies pasteurized milk as far as Bombay, 260 miles away, and makes excellent butter and other processed milk products which are marketed throughout the country. In 1957–58, it purchased milk worth Rs.10,334,697 from about 30,000 individual peasants, all members of village co-operative societies, and most of them owning just one or two she-buffaloes each.

CHAPTER XXIII

AN UNFINISHED REVOLUTION

WHEN Gandhi first returned from South Africa to stay in India, in 1915, he made his headquarters in Gujerat. His *ashram* at Sabarmati later gained world renown. It was from here that the famous "salt march" to the coastal village of Dandi, 200 miles away, was led by him in March 1930 to protest against the salt tax. The march initiated a movement of civil disobedience which convulsed the country periodically for the next few years.[1] Earlier, in 1928, it was in Bardoli in Surat district of Gujerat, that a highly successful agrarian struggle in the form of non-payment of taxes was launched by the peasants under the leadership of Sardar Vallabhbhai Patel.

"It was when the first Bardoli *satyagraha* was being planned in 1921"[2], recalls Kalayanji Mehta,[3] "that Gandhiji asked us how many people in this area would be prepared to sacrifice everything in the civil disobedience movement and to stand by it through thick and thin. He was told 20,000. Then he said, 'only 20,000 out of 80,000! —that is only a quarter?' So we said, 'not really. The population is not eighty thousand, as mentioned in the census, but only 40,000. The rest are *kali praja*.'[4] 'What is that?' Gandhi asked. Then he was told about the tribal population. He was most indignant. 'Oh, so just as the British call us a black people, you call them black. It means half the body is paralysed. How can we fight then?' From

---

[1] The very first experiment in mass *satyagraha* in India, in fact, was also tried out in Gujerat, at Kathlal in the district of Kaira, in February 1918.

[2] It was abandoned later.

[3] One of the earliest associates of Mahatma Gandhi.

[4] Literal meaning: "black people". This is how the tribesmen were described commonly at the time by the *Swarnas*, or caste Hindus. In Surat district, where this incident took place, the Scheduled Tribes constitute 46·7 per cent of the population and Scheduled Castes another 6·5 per cent (*1951 census*).

that day, he advised us to live among the *adivasis*[1] and work to improve their condition, to bring them up to the general level."

Accordingly, soon after that, several *ashrams* were started in *adivasi* villages. They became centres for working out a carefully drafted programme of socio-economic reform, and to them were attached free residential schools with a curriculum adapted to the special background and needs of the tribal people. Social workers in charge were instructed to keep out of politics so that the work could go on uninterruptedly.

There is one of these at Vedachi,[2] for example. The population here is of an *adivasi* tribe, of Choudary. This is one of the oldest *ashrams*, and its impact on the economy and standard of life in the village is marked.[3] Practically all the houses now are the so-called new type, with at least three partitions and tiled roofs, clean and well arranged kitchens, brass utensils, and beds for furniture. Men and women wear the normal Gujerati dress, and not their traditional tribal outfit and bead jewellery. There is a *charkha* in every house, and other village crafts supplement agricultural incomes. Also, thanks to the vigilance of the *ashram* authorities, many of the *adivasis* have benefited from the recent land reforms to become owners of the land they were previously cultivating as mere tenants.

Here at Vedachi I discovered also a unique example of the way in which a dynamic idea can not only move the most ordinary, backward and simple individuals to acts of supreme sacrifice, but can also persuade them to break completely with their traditional past, to adopt new values and patterns of conduct, without the idea being identified directly with any prospect of personal gain or material benefit.

Portrait of a Patriot

Her name is Gainabehen. Short, thin, slight of build, with exquisite features, her skin remarkably fair for a tribeswoman, she is like a delicate piece of china. She must have been pretty when young. She has no teeth now, but a most charming smile and a sweet voice.

---

[1] Another more respectful term for tribes which is now in currency throughout India.

[2] It is also in Surat district.

[3] Members of this tribe, like most tribal people, subsist normally at extremely low levels, not only because of lack of resources, but mainly because of their outlook on life. They will never save. They drink heavily. And they have a "sunset economy" —they worry about providing themselves with necessities of life only for the day. They will not work for more.

As she speaks, she has a way of dropping her eyelids coyly and crossing her small feet or fidgeting with her hands like a shy girl. Her hair is still black and drawn back into a bun. She wears a white sari with a blue border, a white *choli*, and no jewellery except for one white glass bangle. Her husband, Ghuria, is a contrasting study. He is short, squat, dark, heavy-featured, with hair cropped short, a chin unshaven for a week perhaps, and a moustache of no precise shape or character. They also are *Choudary* by caste.

She was married when she was only eleven years old. He was 16. He was a *ghar javayin*, which means that he had to come to live at the girl's house because he was too poor to support her. His village is not far away. But they had not met or seen each other earlier. When her parents died and she separated from her brothers, around 1938, to live independently with her husband and two children, she started out with one *bigha* of land, four *maunds* of *jowar*, five pounds of pulses, one brass *lota*, and one brass *tapali*—a small cooking pot. This was all her dowry and inheritance. The husband had brought nothing, and inherited nothing. His father had no land. "To bring him here, he was given a turban with one rupee and eight annas. That is all."

The first Congress worker with whom she came into contact was Chunnibhai. "He came here for the first time in 1924, I think. I must have been 16 years old then." Chunnibhai used to stay in the village.

"I used to attend his prayer meetings, though my parents used to tell me not to go there. But still I went. I would work the whole day on the land and in the house, and in the evening I felt like attending the prayer meeting.

"Then Gandhiji came to this neighbourhood, in 1927–28 perhaps, and held a meeting near the village." At this meeting he asked who would be prepared to wear *khadi* always, and requested them to raise their hands. "I raised my hand", Gainabehen says, demonstrating how she did it. From that day she became a regular patron of hand-spun and hand-woven cloth and would wear nothing else.

Then came the civil disobedience movement. Gainabehen enrolled herself as a member of the Congress Party and went to picket in Surat town[1] with three other women from this village.

---

[1] As a matter of policy Gandhi used to make a special appeal to women to join in the national struggle. It brought them out in thousands and thereby brought about quicker social reform and improved their position in society more effectively than any acts of law devised to the same end, then or since.

"No, my husband did not give me permission. Nor my own people. But I refused to listen to them." Her voice is low and soft. "My family told me: 'Go if you must, but don't come back. You can go away for good.'"

At Surat the picketers were arrested and then tried. "We were all held guilty and condemned to one year's rigorous imprisonment."

"When the prison term was finished and I arrived at the house, he would not speak to me." She points to Ghuria with a tilt of her head and the constant smile. But they were reconciled and she resumed her routine domestic life.

Then came the turbulent 1942 "Quit India" movement, and she went back to jail in 1943, this time for six months. The charge was that she and another two women attempted to capture a police station at Ulpada, without even a stick in their hands! This time also her husband had opposed her. By now she had four children. She left them all at home and went away.

"When the 15th August 1947 came, I was very happy. We all gathered in the *ashram* to celebrate." Gainabehen wept and fasted when she heard of Mahatma Gandhi's assassination and later of the death of Sardar Patel. She knows that "Nehru is bearing the whole burden of the *raj*."

With the attainment of *swaraj* for which Gainabehen fought so valiantly, she has reverted quietly to obscurity as the wife of a very humble and nondescript peasant. She is no longer in touch with politics or political news. Thanks to the *ashram*, however, all her children went to school. The younger boy is in high school, and the eldest boy has just taken a diploma in civil engineering on a government scholarship. He is probably the first engineer in the whole Choudary tribe. He will naturally go in for service. In trousers, bush coat and spectacles, he represents another generation and a new era.

But for Gainabehen: "I wake up at 4 a.m., light the *chula*, take my bath, wake up the children and say my prayers. Then I go to see the cattle, milk the cows, and take the milk to sell. Yes, I take it myself. . . ." She continues to wear *khadi*, and with hard work and careful husbandry their standard of life has improved considerably.

They now have two bullocks, a cow, a milk-buffalo and two calves and have purchased some more land also, so that they possess six and a half *bighas* instead of the one with which they had started out in life—"all from our own money", she says proudly. In the kitchen

she has a row of glistening brass utensils in place of the two she
received in her dowry.

In Bariya Villages

Despite the examples of Vedachi and Gainabehen, however, the
vast majority of *adivasis* and other backward sections of the population, even in Gujerat,[1] continues as before, not only in their outward
form of dress and habitat, but also in their attitude of general indifference to a higher standard of living, which, naturally, is not con-
ducive to rapid economic growth. For though the "revolution" was
admittedly successful in its immediate objective of attaining political
independence, in its socio-economic aspects it was not complete in
the sense of having permeated equally every stratum, and section of
society.

Thus, in the prosperous *Patidar* villages of Kaira some tenants
and almost all of the agricultural labour population[2] consist largely
of scheduled castes and tribes, of which one of the communities is
known as *Bariya*. It would be difficult to find anywhere, even within
a *Patidar* village, a *Bariya* house made of brick or containing more
than one room shared by humans and cattle—even in instances where
Bariyas own their own land. One can usually tell a *Bariya* field from
a *Patidar* field on merely seeing it from a distance, as also their
animals. The *Bariya* buffalo yields less milk than that of the *Patidar*.[3]
The *Bariya* in Kaira continues to be basically a subsistence cultivator.

---

[1] They constitute about 25 per cent of the total population.

[2] In Gujerat as a whole 42·9 per cent of the total rural families are classed as
owner-cultivators; 22·5 per cent are tenants and 15 per cent are agricultural
labourers (1950–51).

[3] According to a survey carried out in village Lambhvel, in Anand *taluk* of
Kaira district, tenants and labourers who constituted 47 per cent of the total agricultural families owned about 25 per cent of the total number of buffaloes in the
village. "The buffaloes owned by such families also yield relatively less milk *per
capita*. Their share in the total village milk production is even less than 20 per cent.
It is, therefore, safe to generalize that the contribution of these classes in the total
village milk supply is made at relatively less efficiency, whether it is due to the low
qualities of buffaloes or it is due to bad feeding."
Then again, in relation to the Kaira Milk Producers' Co-operative Union
described earlier, tenants and labourers constituting 47 per cent of all the families
accounted for a mere 17 per cent of the total membership of its feeder Co-operative
Milk Producers' Society in the same village. Only 23 per cent of the tenant families
and 7·5 per cent from among the labourers have joined the Co-operative. A similar
survey in Gopalpura village showed the same results. (*Problems in Capital Accumu-
lation by the Tenant in the Ryotwari Area of Kaira District*, 1950, by N. K. Desai
& S. G. Madiman, Institute of Agriculture, Anand, 1951.)

Village Dhathi has 40 houses, all of *Bariyas*, and every family owns land. Five to seven acres is the average holding. It has a primary school—a single-storied mud house, like all the houses. The houses are in straight rows, with buffaloes tied in front of them in the lane during the day and inside the houses at night. No one has apparently ever thought of emigrating elsewhere, even a few miles away. "We have too strong ties with the village. We can never even think of leaving it. To emigrate it requires cleverness which we have not got", says Amar Shah.

"How can we go; where are we to go?", asks Birjibhai. There is not a single bicycle in the village, and only three bullock carts, one of which is broken. There is no spinning, weaving or any processing industry of any kind. Nor is there a single irrigation pump. Men never bring cash home, but cloth, salt and spices, for which they barter the little cotton they produce. The rest of the land is all under food crops, none of which are marketed.

It is the same in Magrol, also a *Bariya* village, in the Charotar area. All the peasants have land, but still their mud huts are the same as they were 60 or perhaps 600 years ago. The political "revolution" has obviously failed to have any impact on them as it had on the *Patidars*, their immediate neighbours.

The Two Prayer Meetings

Similarly in Sewagram, where Mahatma Gandhi spent the latter part of his life:[1]

"*Bapu Kuti*"[2], says the board outside a bamboo fence. We enter by a gate. There are some *neem* trees and flowering bushes along the fence; on the ground is just plain gravel. Inside the mud hut, near the entrance, are *Bapu's* wooden sandals and walking stick in a locked glass case. The hut has a mud floor, mud plastered walls (bamboo inside), a white covered mattress and back rest on the floor where he used to sit and work, three small tables—everything as it used to be. The rest of his possessions—the spinning wheel, paper-weights (plain stones of various shapes and sizes), the three monkeys, ink stand, rosary—are locked in another glass case. There is bamboo

---

[1] Gandhi ceased to be a member of the Indian National Congress in 1934. Thereafter, his intimate personal connections with Gujerat more or less ceased. Sewagram became his headquarters from 1936. It was then situated in the State of Madhya Pradesh. Now it is in the State of Maharashtra.

[2] *Bapu* means father. It is one of the appellations by which Gandhi was and still is commonly referred to. *Kuti* means cottage.

matting on the floor for visitors to sit on. Famous quotations, hand written, hang on the walls. All is silence, empty. Outside, the walls are covered with dry date-palm leaves, like other village houses in this area, for protection against the heavy monsoon rain.

Now many buildings in the *ashram* are lying vacant, though the Kasturba Hospital is here and the *ashram* is the headquarters of the *Hindustani Talim Sangh*. This organization heads the movement for "basic education", first devised by Gandhi as a cheaper and more suitable system for a poor country like India. There is a training centre for teachers and pre-basic, basic and post-basic schools also. The *ashram* works its own fields, raises its food requirements, and the boys in school have to work for their fees on the lines laid down by Gandhi. Prayers are held in the evening as usual—under the *peepul* tree planted by *Bapu* himself in 1936, just outside his cottage compound. A white cushion with a back rest is kept for him; the audience sits facing it in rows, on the ground, on small mats— women to the left.

There is a hush, as silent figures walk in to join the small con- gregation. It has become dark, but there is a light in *Bapu's* hut. Will he walk out? The prayers have started; his favourite hymn is being sung. I cannot resist turning repeatedly to look at the hut, almost expecting him to emerge from the door any moment, walk out and take his seat. But the song is half way through. He still has not come. In the monsoon sky there is only a smudge for the young moon. There are no stars. Dark faces merge in the darkness. Only the white shirts stand out and the white *chandani* flowers on the bush near the fence of the cottage. The prayers are ending. They are singing the final prayer song. I pause, strain to hear *Bapu's* voice, always out of tune, his bald head bowed. He never missed singing "*Raghupati Raghava Raja Ram*". Tears stream down my face. . . .

And then it is over. In a matter of moments everyone has dis- persed. Once again there is only silence and darkness, except for the glimmer of the hurricane lantern inside the hut.

Immediately after the prayers at the *ashram*, however, there is another prayer meeting in Sewagram village to which the *ashram* is attached. Here over 100 *Mahar*[1] families have adopted Buddhism in the last two years. A Japanese *bhikku*, Rev. Saiji Makino, who does veterinary work at the *ashram*, conducts their prayers. He walks all the way from the *ashram* beating on a fan-like skin drum with a

---

[1] Scheduled caste.

detachable handle. It has Japanese letters painted on it in black. He wears ankle-length boots with his saffron robe; his face and head are clean shaven. He has come from Japan, in search of truth in the land of the Buddha.

Rev. Makino and I go to what used to be the *Harijan* quarter of the village. A young boy and a couple of men come to receive the *bhikku* with a lantern near the entrance to the village. A white ceramic statue of the Buddha, made in Japan, is kept on a rough wooden crate in the small one-room hut of an agricultural labourer, Shivanath. The room is lit by a lantern. The temple to house the statue has been under construction for more than two years, but only the brick walls are up; the roof is still lacking. It was begun as a Hindu temple, but then the idols were thrown into the river and it was designated to become a Buddhist place of worship. The whole group of neo-Buddhists in Sewagram is helping to build it but they are short of funds and do not know how to complete it. Already the exposed walls are cracking.

Above the statue in Shivanath's house is a coloured photograph of the late Dr. Ambedkar and his wife. It was Ambedkar who started the movement, which is fairly strong in Maharashtra, to encourage *Harijans* to leave the Hindu fold altogether and become Buddhists to escape untouchability and the lowly position accorded them in Hindu society.[1] A scholar and one of the framers of the Indian Constitution, Ambedkar himself was a *Harijan* from Maharashtra who embraced Buddhism.

In front of Buddha's statue is a bowl full of water and incense is burning. The room is crowded. The congregation consists mostly of boys and young men; I see only one old man. Many of them are ex-students of Sewagram *ashram* school. Two of them are still working there. The *bhikku* conducts the prayers in Japanese. The drums are distributed to all present, and they beat time and repeat mechanically what the *bhikku* says. Later he turns his back to the statue to face his audience and tries to explain in very broken Hindi the meaning of the prayer. It is difficult to understand him.

After the prayers are over, we talk. The people present in the room express only unalloyed, violent bitterness. Neither the spirit of

---

[1] They are known as neo-Buddhists. In almost every instance their conversion has upset the village economy because they refuse to perform now their customary menial tasks, like disposing of the carcasses of dead animals, and so on. This results in acute tensions and often violence between them and the upper caste population in the villages.

Gandhi nor that of the Buddha is here; only resentment, hatred and suspicion.

In *Bapu's* time there used to be a *charkha* in every home in Sewagram. Today, there is not a single spinning wheel in the whole village. No one wears *khadi*, except those who work in the *ashram*; for them it is compulsory. Nor do the villagers attend the prayer meetings at the *ashram*, which they always did when Gandhi was alive.

As for "basic education", of which Sewagram *ashram* is the centre, they say with unconcealed contempt: "We do not send our children to the *ashram* school beyond the fourth class (i.e. primary), because those who pass out of "*nai talim*"[1] cannot get jobs. So our boys go to Wardha town; they walk the four miles to study in a conventional school. They have to leave early in the morning to reach it on time."

"We don't want to remain tillers of the soil for ever. We also want to become lawyers and doctors. '*Nai talim*' is no good for that", is their explanation.

Saddest of all, the village is riven into two hostile blocs, one of caste-Hindus and the other of Buddhists who were previously *Harijans*. There is complete segregation and social boycott between them. There has been no improvement in the status of the *Harijans* since they embraced a new religion. They continue to be treated as untouchables. And where in Gandhi's time the two sections had lived in amity and oneness, since he was insistent on abolition of untouchability and caste distinctions, there is bitter and open antagonism now, which extends even to the precincts of the *ashram* school. No work is done together. "Therefore we have made no progress in development work or anything", I am told, though the village is covered now by the Community Development programme. "Our economic condition is very poor; worse than what it used to be."[2]

Obviously, though the "revolution" came to Sewagram under the personal direction of Gandhi himself, it has proved to be of a wholly transient character. Almost everything that was achieved in the

---

[1] Literally, "new education". It is another name for basic education. It was primarily for the rural poor that Gandhi evolved this system of "new education", in which craft and manual work is given special emphasis. It is oriented to village background and needs, the idea being that the student will continue to live in the village when he grows up and do agriculture like his father.

[2] This may be due to the loss of income from spinning and other village crafts which were such a prominent feature of the "Gandhian economy".

village in Gandhi's time in the social and economic fields is lost already, in less than a decade after his death.

By morning light, in physical appearance also, Sewagram is exactly the same today as any other village in the area—drab mud walls, dirty lanes with cattle, bullock cart wheels and manure and dirt heaps everywhere. On a small mound of refuse, however, stands a little dark-skinned girl, in a frock once white, now dirty and ripped at the right shoulder, hanging loosely on a very thin body down to the shins. With short curly hair matted and uncombed, tousled by the monsoon wind, her eyes crinkled, her small round face overrun with laughter, she is clapping and waving her grubby hands in sheer delight. A blossom in the dust. . . .

THE LAST CHAPTER

CHAPTER XXIV

SOME CONCLUSIONS AND QUESTIONS

I

So ends the story.

It is, of course, an incomplete story, as any account of a human society must always be. Moreover, though I travelled, talked and listened for a whole year, I could meet only a minute fraction of India's immense population. And even of what I saw and recorded, only a small portion could be included in this volume.

The book gives, therefore, only a few glimpses really of the conditions in which some of the peasant communities live and work, and of those of their attitudes, beliefs and aspirations, which to my mind are important to the success of the many development programmes and projects now under way in the country's rural areas. In so far as matters of policy are concerned, it raises questions, but does not provide the answers to them.

The reader will find many pertinent issues missing from my talks with the villagers—as for example, the question of limiting the size of their families. I did talk about it on several occasions. But almost invariably I found that the problem does not exist yet on the personal level in the minds of the people I spoke to. Villagers do not worry much about the number of children they have, no matter how poor they might be. Not to have any issue is considered to be a much greater disaster than to have too many.

Similarly, the impact of co-operative farming and of various kinds of service co-operatives providing marketing facilities, etc. has not been dealt with fully in the text. Except perhaps in the field of credit, the co-operative movement is still in its early infancy in the country, in the experimental stage. Moreover, here again, though it is the official policy to pattern the future organization of all economic life in the rural areas on co-operation, there is little understanding yet of its principles or appreciation of its potentialities among the peasant communities. Normally, whenever I broached the subject, and I did so in every village I went to, the spontaneous reaction was one of indifference and often indeed, of distrust, ridicule or hostility to the very idea, especially to that of joint-farming.

Nor have I given an account of the work of the thousands of officials at different levels of responsibility who are engaged in administering and implementing the development policies and projects in the rural areas, and of their relations with the village people. The subject is interesting and important. I have, however, not dealt with it directly in this volume, as I have also not tried to assess or evaluate specific government programmes, except in so far as their impact on a community is revealed occasionally in the attitudes and opinions expressed by some of its members.

With all these and other limitations the author hopes, nevertheless, to have conveyed to the reader a fair idea of the tremendous diversity of the problems that economic planning must face in this country's rural sector. In recent years the planners have increasingly urged that differences in physical conditions, such as climate, man/land ratio, soil, irrigation, communications, must be given greater recognition in the framing and location of schemes to increase agricultural production. After talking to the peasants all over the country, however, I came to the conclusion that the problem of material resources is only one of several factors that must be taken into consideration and to which any programme designed to raise farm yields must be adjusted. And it is not always the most important. A community's attitude to work can be a more decisive determinant for raising productivity in Indian agriculture than material resources, or for that matter even technology. What is more, this attitude to work, as we have seen, differs widely between regions and communities.

The district of Tanjore, for instance, is richly endowed by way of natural resources and irrigation facilities. But the peasant in the adjacent district of Coimbatore, though the natural conditions there are not so favourable, is known to be a more efficient agriculturist than the man in Tanjore, because he is a better worker and is prepared to exert himself more. It is highly probable, therefore, that given even less facilities, the Coimbatore farmer would show better response and higher achievements in increasing production than the *mirasdar* of Tanjore.

Throughout India, in fact, the best farmers are to be found not necessarily in communities most favourably endowed with material resources, but in those that are traditionally agriculturist by caste, such as the *Sadgops* in West Bengal, the *Jats* in the Punjab and the *Patidars* in Gujerat. It is so mainly because these castes have an inherited respect for agricultural work and they are not precluded by religion or tradition from working on the land. The result is that even if members of these "professionally agricultural" communities have been reduced to the status of tenants or landless labourers, they will be found superior in husbandry to the non-working castes of landowners, such as *Brahmins*, *Rajputs*, *Banias*, etc., though the latter may have more capital, land, education, and thus superior means to acquire modern techniques and tools of cultivation.

It is not only in their attitude to manual work that the peasant communities differ. There are significant differences also in respect of other traits and aptitudes, such as thrift, industry, mobility and readiness to exploit economic opportunity, which makes the problem of planning even more complicated. It is clear from the many examples in the text of this book that there is no uniformity yet in the prevailing value systems which determine not only a community's pattern of production and consumption, of farm management, marketing and even housing, but also its primary attitudes and wants. These vary greatly from one community to the next, within groups in the same region and even locality otherwise enjoying in all respects equal resources and opportunities.

In the absence of common valuations, a uniform response to common incentives and stimuli cannot be expected. On the other hand, variations in the value system can make all the difference to the extent of success or failure of a development scheme independently of the material and natural resources. They can also defeat the central purpose of many of the reforms, policies and programmes —for instance, the land reforms—which are centrally framed for universal and uniform application to all rural communities throughout the country.

On the operational plane at least, planners and economists tend to overlook this lack of consensus on economic values. It is assumed— even if it is seldom explicitly stated—that given equal opportunity, financial incentive and resources, all communities will respond, and respond similarly, in their productive efforts and economic achievements.

I need only to point, however, to the striking variations I found in response to one of the oldest and most elementary techniques in use in agriculture, namely irrigation. Irrigating of crops is by no means a twentieth century invention. Nor is it a borrowed concept. It has been in practice in parts of India as long as history. And though modern technology may be utilized now in the construction of the new irrigation projects, there is little or no change in the actual method of irrigating the fields.

Yet compare the differences in attitude towards irrigation of the peasants in Coimbatore in Madras, Raichur in Mysore, Kurnool in Andhra, Gaya in Bihar, Edna Kalaska in the Punjab and Kaira in Gujerat. Compare also the differences of the three communities of Pradhanatikara, Budelpali and Champaparda, all within the one district of Sambalpur in Orissa, in their response to the Hirakud irrigation project. These differences were not due to variations in administrative efficiency in distributing the water, or to differences in material resources or in the educational equipment of the peasants. They had much deeper roots in traditional beliefs and attitudes, such as those to work, to surplus production, and to diet. In terms of planning, the result of these differences is that at the end of the Second Five Year Plan period in 1961 some three and a half million acres of irrigable land remained unirrigated. Of the irrigated area only 12 per cent was under double cropping.

2

With all the diversity in their value systems, however, there appears to be one characteristic which is strikingly common to almost all the rural communities, and which again is highly pertinent to planning. It pertains to the peasants' attitude to their standard of living and to its improvement.

If democratic planning is to succeed and result in a continuous and self-sustaining process of economic growth, obviously there must be a corresponding and urgent desire in the community as a whole for its fruit in the form of a rising standard of consumption. Planning in India is framed on the assumption—which in view of the extreme poverty of the people would seem logical—that the desire for higher levels of living is inherent and more or less universal among the masses being planned for. According to this assumption, every prevailing standard of life becomes minimal as a base for further progress.

From what I have seen and experienced, however, it would seem that a great majority of the rural communities do not share in this concept of an ever-rising standard of living. The upper level they are prepared to strive for is limited and it is the floor generally that is bottomless. This does not mean that the desired standard is always fixed at the subsistence level. It varies with different communities. In some groups it is very much higher than in others, and it may be considerably more than the minimum necessary to breed and survive. But whatever the level, it tends to be static, with a ceiling rather than a floor, and it is socially determined. Generally, the lower the level, the more static the aspirations tend to be.

If my observation is correct, it largely invalidates one of the principal assumptions on which present planning for economic development in the rural sector is based. For in a situation of limited and static aspirations, if a man should feel that his requirements are just two bags of paddy per year, he works for two bags but not for more. If he looks to the stars, it is only to worship them, not to pluck them. To that extent his poverty may be, and often is, unnecessary and his productivity lower than his circumstances and the resources available to him would permit. In fact, often, the peasant does not consider it moral to want more, as is clear from the statements we have recorded of tenants and landless labourers in the eastern districts of Andhra. Nor is Balappa of Raichur, who chooses to stop work at mid-day despite his extreme poverty, by any means a solitary example of individual eccentricity.

Many consequences flow from this phenomenon of "limited" aspirations. Unless a man feels the desire to have more material wealth *sufficiently to strive for it*, he cannot be expected to have much interest in new techniques; there will be little attempt on his part to innovate. He may and often does disdain to engage in activities yielding the highest net advantage even within the available opportunities and the restrictions imposed on him by the society to which he belongs. And where an extraneous factor like the introduction of irrigation brings about higher incomes, the increase may be wasted in non-essential forms of consumption instead of being invested further to maximize production—as we saw in the case of the peasants in Mandya and of the Bagdis in the Gang canal region.

3

What then is the conclusion?

There is, of course, no question in the Indian context as to the need for state planning for economic development.

Nor do I discount the possibility of bringing about an impressive

N

increase in total production as well as in the national and per capita income by means of heavy capital investments, modern techniques, and efficient administration.

But in planning for the farming community it is apparent that there cannot be any economics in isolation from sociology and social psychology. There are many causal relationships and connections between purely economic factors and social and cultural conditions which cannot be ignored or excluded from economic analysis and planning.

Each of India's millions of agricultural holdings is an autonomous unit of production and must remain so. Production in agriculture will therefore continue to be the ultimate and individual responsibility of over 70 million peasants. It will inevitably be conditioned by their inner motivations and attitudes, most of which, as we have seen, are still rooted in or identified with religious belief and an obsolete tradition, are not integrated in a common value system, and are largely paralysed by limited aspirations.

In these circumstances, introduction of new techniques from outside will help only to a limited extent. Unless the desire for change and for appreciably higher living standards takes root in the peasant communities these techniques will often not be accepted or exploited fully—as has been the case with the Japanese method of paddy cultivation for example. This technique was introduced in the paddy growing areas about a decade ago. But rarely has it been adopted in its entirety anywhere. The average yield of rice at 906 pounds per acre (in 1960–61) continues to be the lowest in the world.

Even after some progress is achieved, there will be danger of stabilization at every new level of "induced prosperity". The peasants may continue to depend, as now, on the initiative, resources and pressures from external agencies for being driven to further progress. There may be thus, as there have been in the past, recurring periods of stagnation even if they be at somewhat higher technological levels.

There will not be any spectacular improvement in the basic situation. The fundamental problem of increasing the economic effectiveness and efficiency with which cultivation is conducted may still remain. Development will not become a self-generating process with its own momentum unless the value system of the community, and the social structure containing it, are first altered and adjusted to be in harmony with the socio-economic objectives of planning.

As we have seen, even now certain communities do not require much persuasion to adopt new techniques. In fact, they do not always wait for the government extension agencies to teach them or to extend to them various financial incentives and facilities by way of loans and subsidies. There are others, and they probably form the majority, who, in spite of the efforts of the extension agencies and the inducements offered by them, seem inert and indifferent. They pass up repeated opportunities to increase production and income, even when opportunity knocks at their very door. This is correlated with the respective value systems of those communities and the individual peasant's place in the village society.

The major question that we face then is this.

If it is accepted that in rural India the social factor, taken in its comprehensive sense, is one of the primary determinants of economic underdevelopment and development, will it not be necessary to try to induce the relevant social change also in as planned, precise, calculated and integrated a manner as economic change, to a greater extent and much more effectively than is being attempted at present?

If so, when a development scheme is projected, the relevant social and psychological attributes of each community will need to be studied and examined in the same intensive manner as an inventory of the physical resources is made at present. On the basis of such studies means will have to be found for bringing about the necessary changes in people's attitudes and behaviour and the beliefs underlying them. These means and methods will have to be within the framework and in keeping with the general policy and principles of democratic planning.

The only escape from such a course would be to believe that a predominantly physical, institutional and financial approach in planning, concerned primarily with the engineering aspect of increasing the stock of real capital and improvement of technology, could be relied upon to evolve a chain of new human relationships and patterns of economic behaviour suited to its purpose.

In the conditions that prevail in rural India, however, would it be reasonable to expect that the "side effects" of physical, institutional and economic development will bring about the necessary adjustments in the human factor more or less automatically with the help simply of the demonstrations and exhortations of the extension services provided under the Community Development programme?

Can we really expect that such a revolutionary transformation will come by itself, when it has not been possible to enforce even simple acts of social legislation, such as removal of untouchability or raising the marriage age of girls and boys? Are there any signs or trends in the rural areas on a significant enough scale to confirm such expectations?

Even if we should grant that this would happen in the long run, is there any assurance that the traditional values and attitudes will be changed in this manner into the desired ones, to the requisite extent, at the crucial points and with the necessary speed? Will there not be too great a time lag, and will that not be dangerous, particularly in view of the high rate of increase in population? The time factor is of utmost importance.

On a more fundamental level, the question arises whether, in the agricultural field, new techniques, tools and institutions can be made effective within the existing framework and environment. Can, for instance, the mere introduction of model institutions, such as *panchayats* or farming co-operatives, be expected to break up and destroy the caste basis of the prevailing structure of power, property, influence and status and create a more egalitarian and flexible social organization within the village communities? Though since 1947, India has enacted perhaps more land reform legislation than any other country in the world, it has not succeeded in changing in any essentials the power pattern, the deep economic disparities, nor the traditional hierarchical nature of inter-group relationships which govern the economic life of village society.

To what extent can we rely upon the spread of education to alter the situation radically and suitably for development? Is it not a fact that at present, far from eradicating any of the problems, education seems mostly to bypass them in the rural areas, and, in fact, to introduce fresh ones. There are a few exceptions. But, generally, the educated son of a peasant, though he may own sufficient land, seeks alternative avenues of work which he considers to be less difficult, more pleasant and more dignified, even though his income from them may be lower than what he could earn if he worked on the land. Indeed he prefers to remain idle than work on the land, because that to him is wholly incompatible with education.

There is also the fact to consider that within the village the individual is never detached and thrown into new and different surroundings of abstract and impersonal relationships which can be expected to emancipate him and compel his transformation, distorted or otherwise, as happens when he moves into an industrial area or a large city.

The basic problem, therefore, of how to bring about rapid change in a people's social and economic values within the framework of democratic planning, remains. It requires fresh thinking, and is a challenge to the government, the politicians, the social scientists and the economists engaged in planning in India. It is a difficult problem. But it should not be an impossible one. Given the will, there seems to be no reason why it should not be possible to tackle it. I can clearly assert that the experience of my travels and contacts with the village communities has not given me any sense of pessimism or defeatism.

An essential condition of finding a solution, however, is that the problem be first recognized, understood and faced squarely in all its aspects and implications, however much these may conflict with existing theories and preconceptions.

GLOSSARY OF HINDI WORDS

Ahar, irrigation reservoir.

Ahimsa, non-violence.

Ambar Charkha, hand-operated spinning wheel with four spindles.

Andheri, dust storm.

Angarkha, a short coat with flared skirt; traditional dress of men mainly in Rajasthan and parts of Gujerat.

Angithi, brazier burning charcoal.

Anna, coin; sixteenth part of a rupee.

Ashram, usually a centre where a community dedicated to a common cause lives and works together.

Bajra, pearl millet.

Bania, of Vaisya caste; engages primarily in business. The word is also used to describe a grocery shop keeper.

Batai, share-cropping.

Begar, compulsory free labour which peasants were under obligation to provide to the landlord or the State.

Bhag, fate.

Bhangi, belongs to one of the untouchable castes; employed to clean toilets and perform other such menial jobs.

Bhangin, female of *bhangi*.

Bhikku, Buddhist monk.

Bidi, cigarette in which the tobacco is rolled in leaves instead of paper. They are very cheap and are smoked mostly by villagers and the urban poor.

Bigha, in most villages land is measured in terms of the *bigha*, but its extent varies from State to State. Its equivalent in each case in terms of a standard acre has therefore been given in a footnote.

Bodhi, a *peepul* tree; *Ficus religiosa*.

Chabutra, platform.

Chaddar, shawl.

Chakki, hand-worked millstone for grinding corn.

Chana, gram; chick-pea or pulse generally.

Chula, open stove made of brick and earth on which cooking is done in Indian homes.

Deodar, a cedar of the Himalayas; *cedrus deodara*.

Dhoti, one of the most common of Indian male garments.

Diva, a little earthen oil lamp.

Diwali, Hindu festival of lights.

Doli, palanquin.

Gaddi, a shepherd community in north India.

Gud, brown, unrefined sugar made from sugar cane juice.

Harijan, the untouchable or one of the scheduled castes as classified in the Indian Constitution.

Hat, market; usually held once a week for a group of villages.

Hookah, water tobacco-pipe.

Jaggery, coarse dark sugar made from sugar cane or palm-sap.

Jai Hind, means "hail India". It is also used as a form of salutation.

Jhuming, shifting cultivation.

Jowar, millet.

Kahar, sub-caste of Sudras.

Kaharin, female of *kahar*.

Karandi and Kudal, mason's trowel and tray used in laying foundation stones.

Katcheri, law court.

Khadi/Khaddar, handspun and handwoven cloth.

Kharif, monsoon crop.

Khud, valley or depression.

Kisan, peasant.

Kurta, Indian-style shirt.

Kutcha, opposite of *pucca*; used to describe mud walls or roads and floors without a hard surface.

Langty, loin-cloth.

Lota, small brass vessel used for carrying water.

Lungi, male garment worn mainly in south India; like a sarong.

Makki, maize.

Malik, master.

Maund, weight measure equivalent to 82·28 lbs.

Moser, death feast.

Moth, an inferior grain.

Mukhia, means chief. In Bihar it is used as a title for the president of a *panchayat*.

Neem, an evergreen tree; *Azadirachta indica*.

Palki, palanquin.

Panchayat, village council.

Panchayat Ghar, office building for a *panchayat*.

Peepul, large fig tree; *Ficus religiosa*.

Pice, coin; one-fourth of an anna.

Prakriti, nature or natural laws.

Pucca, means solid. Also used to describe any structure made of brick or concrete.

Pukka Khana, certain varieties of cooked food permitted on occasions when members of different castes eat together.

Purkhas, elders.

Purohit, priest.

Rabi, winter crop.

Raghupati Raghava Raja Ram, favourite prayer song of Mahatma Gandhi.

Ragi, millet.

Raj, literal meaning, kingdom. Also means government.

Roti, Indian-style unleavened bread, flat and round.

Rupee, major denomination of Indian currency.

Russibundi, meaning "Russianism", or the Russian system or way of life.

Ryot, peasant.

Ryotwari, system of peasant proprietorship.

Sadhu, religious mendicant.

Sag, leafy vegetable.

Sarpanch, president of *panchayat.*

Satyagraha, non-violent civil disobedience—technique of fighting for political and other rights made famous by Mahatma Gandhi.

Shamiana, a canvas enclosure.

Shira, a sweet drink.

Shramdan, voluntary free labour, usually for some community project.

Shuddhi, purification ritual.

Swamijee, holy man.

Swaraj, independence.

Taccavi, government loans to farmers.

Tehmat, resembles *lungi;* worn by men mainly in the Punjab.

Til, small grain; also yields edible oil.

Vikas, means development; also used to describe the department responsible for community development in rural areas.